Zebra

Animal
Series editor: Jonathan Burt

Already published

Albatross Graham Barwell · *Ant* Charlotte Sleigh · *Ape* John Sorenson · *Badger* Daniel Heath Justice
Bat Tessa Laird · *Bear* Robert E. Bieder · *Beaver* Rachel Poliquin · *Bee* Claire Preston · *Beetle* Adam Dodd
Bison Desmond Morris · *Camel* Robert Irwin · *Cat* Katharine M. Rogers · *Chicken* Annie Potts
Cockroach Marion Copeland · *Cow* Hannah Velten · *Crocodile* Dan Wylie · *Crow* Boria Sax
Deer John Fletcher · *Dog* Susan McHugh · *Dolphin* Alan Rauch · *Donkey* Jill Bough
Duck Victoria de Rijke · *Eagle* Janine Rogers · *Eel* Richard Schweid · *Elephant* Dan Wylie
Falcon Helen Macdonald · *Flamingo* Caitlin R. Kight · *Fly* Steven Connor · *Fox* Martin Wallen
Frog Charlotte Sleigh · *Giraffe* Edgar Williams · *Goat* Joy Hinson · *Gorilla* Ted Gott and
Kathryn Weir · *Guinea Pig* Dorothy Yamamoto · *Hare* Simon Carnell · *Hedgehog* Hugh Warwick
Hippopotamus Edgar Williams · *Horse* Elaine Walker · *Hyena* Mikita Brottman · *Kangaroo* John Simons
Leech Robert G. W. Kirk and Neil Pemberton · *Leopard* Desmond Morris · *Lion* Deirdre Jackson
Lizard Boria Sax · *Llama* Helen Cowie · *Lobster* Richard J. King · *Monkey* Desmond Morris
Moose Kevin Jackson · *Mosquito* Richard Jones · *Moth* Matthew Gandy · *Mouse* Georgie Carroll
Octopus Richard Schweid · *Ostrich* Edgar Williams · *Otter* Daniel Allen · *Owl* Desmond Morris
Oyster Rebecca Stott · *Parrot* Paul Carter · *Peacock* Christine E. Jackson · *Penguin* Stephen Martin
Pig Brett Mizelle · *Pigeon* Barbara Allen · *Rabbit* Victoria Dickenson · *Rat* Jonathan Burt
Rhinoceros Kelly Enright · *Salmon* Peter Coates · *Scorpion* Louise M. Pryke · *Seal* Victoria Dickenson
Shark Dean Crawford · *Sheep* Philip Armstrong · *Skunk* Alyce Miller · *Snail* Peter Williams
Snake Drake Stutesman · *Sparrow* Kim Todd · *Spider* Katarzyna and Sergiusz Michalski
Swallow Angela Turner · *Swan* Peter Young · *Tiger* Susie Green · *Tortoise* Peter Young
Trout James Owen · *Vulture* Thom van Dooren · *Walrus* John Miller and Louise Miller
Whale Joe Roman · *Wild Boar* Dorothy Yamamoto · *Woodpecker* Gerard Gorman · *Wolf* Garry Marvin
Zebra Christopher Plumb and Samuel Shaw

Zebra

Christopher Plumb and Samuel Shaw

REAKTION BOOKS

For friends and family (because we too are herd animals)

Published by
REAKTION BOOKS LTD
Unit 32, Waterside
44–48 Wharf Road
London N1 7UX, UK
www.reaktionbooks.co.uk

First published 2018
Copyright © Christopher Plumb and Samuel Shaw 2018

Printed and bound in China by 1010 Printing International Ltd

A catalogue record for this book is available from the British Library

ISBN 978 1 78023 935 4

Contents

Introduction: Defining the Zebra

One of the last animals to appear in the dictionary – clocking in just before the zebu – it is usually the fate of the zebra to find itself at the end of things, closing the narrative started by the aardvark. In Thomas Pennant's *History of Quadrupeds* (1781), however, the zebra makes its appearance relatively early on, riding on the coattails of its illustrious equid cousins. At the time Pennant was writing, non-African audiences were still getting to grips with the animal; nevertheless, his description covers most of the major responses that zebras have evoked over the last few hundred years, revealing an animal of distinctly contradictory qualities:

> H.[orse] with a short erect mane. That, the head, and body are striped downwards with lines of brown, on a pale buff ground: the legs and thighs striped cross-ways. Tail like that of an ass, furnished with long hairs at the end. Size of a common mule.
>
> This most elegant of quadrupeds: inhabits from *Congo* and *Angola*, across *Africa*, to *Abyssinia*, and southward as low as the *Cape*. Inhabit the plains, but on sight of men, run into the woods and disappear. Are gregarious, vicious, untameable, useless: vastly swift: is called by the *Portuguese*, *Burro di Matto*, or wild ass.

Made for monochrome? Thomas Bewick, *Zebra*, 1799, wood engraving.

Will couple with the ass. A he-ass was brought to a female zebra kept a few years ago in *London*. The *zebra* at first refused any commerce with it: the ass was then painted, to resemble the exotic animal. The strategem took effect, and she admitted its embraces; and produced a mule.[1]

In this passage, Pennant lays out the main attractions of, objections to and possible uses of the zebra that dominate subsequent discourse. The animal is, above all, considered beautiful: 'the most elegant of quadrupeds' in Pennant's words (a description that surely derives from the Comte de Buffon's *Natural History*, in which the handsomeness of the zebra was first noted). Forty years later, the naturalist William Burchell, encountering a herd of ten zebras in southern Africa, described them as

the most beautifully marked animals I had ever seen: their clean sleek limbs glittered in the sun, and the brightness and regularity of their striped coat, presented a picture of extraordinary beauty, in which probably they are not surpassed by any quadruped.[2]

It is clear that few animals are more pleasing to the eye, which goes some way towards explaining the zebra's attraction for artists, especially those working in monochrome media, for which the zebra was especially well designed. The Spanish wildlife photographer Marina Cano, who has worked with many animals, recently noted,

I've not yet found an animal more photogenic than zebras . . . Their physiognomy and coloring are spectacular. Unlike almost any other animal, they're simultaneously concrete and abstract. Any angle is good.[3]

Indeed, one theory of the origin of the word zebra (which dates back to the beginning of the sixteenth century) is that it comes from the Hebrew word *tzìbi*, meaning 'beauty'.[4] For the Karamojong people, based in northeast Uganda, zebras are 'the epitome of beauty', a view shared by many other African communities (though not those for whom the zebra is better seen either as a source of good meat or as a pest).[5] Such beauty can prove irresistible. During a recent interview with the nature writer Charles Foster, journalist Simon Hattenstone encountered a zebra skin hung up on the wall of his lounge, a souvenir from Foster's hunting days, the memory of which now haunts him. Why would a man still display a hunting trophy if he regretted his shooting days? 'But it's so beautiful,' answered Foster.[6] Foster's response is regularly echoed in contemporary culture, in which once-unfashionable

Any angle is good: three plains zebras drinking at a waterhole.

9

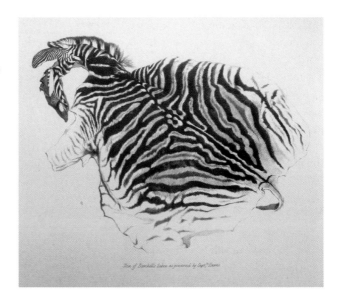

Zebra skin, from William Cornwallis Harris, *Portraits of the Game and Wild Animals of Southern Africa* (1840).

traditions such as taxidermy are making a distinct comeback, uneasy colonial connotations brushed aside on account of an object's perceived beauty. No longer the preserve of the trophy-hunter, zebra heads can now be found on the walls of hip restaurants and chic apartments in cities such as New York, London and Paris.[7]

The zebra has never ceased to be a spectacle, however familiar its form has become. In April 2015 three zebras bolted from a farm in Brussels, while in November two absconded from a circus in Philadelphia. Both escapes made international headlines and created significant social-media buzz, not because they caused any major disruption, but because the sight of zebras galloping through a city centre remains thrilling, almost otherworldly. The ubiquitous panda may be the world's favourite black-and-white animal; nevertheless, the zebra comfortably qualifies as an example of 'charismatic megafauna' (the term used for animals considered to be among the most distinctive and/or cute). The word 'zebra', in fact, now extends far beyond equids, and is commonly used as shorthand to refer to any animal with black-and-white markings (including the zebra finch, zebrafish, zebra mussels, zebra spider, zebra shark and zebra caterpillar). Zebra print competes strongly against leopard and tiger print in the animal-print popularity stakes, and can be found on almost anything, from beanbags to bikinis, car seats to pencil cases. Such popularity comes, of course, at a high price: the trade for authentic zebra skins continues to be a significant factor in population decline. Fame and beauty, as ever, excuse all sorts of crimes.

There's nothing quite like a zebra – except, of course, there is. For all the beauty of their distinctive and scientifically puzzling black-and-white stripes (which, as Pennant observes, often

The 'convict' or 'zebra' cichlid (*Amatitlania nigrofasciata*).

accommodate a certain amount of brown), zebras share many qualities with animals not normally associated with the word 'elegant'. Pennant alludes to this when noting that the zebra's tail is 'like that of an ass' and that it is the size 'of a common mule'. He even suggests that a painted donkey could pass for a zebra (a popular ruse throughout history, as it happens). In 1763 the Reverend John Kidgell composed a short fable on a similar theme:

> A zebra, distinguished by the beautiful variegation of his birth-day suit, was so insolently vain of it, as to look upon the whole levee with contempt. 'Silly sop', says an Arabian courser [a fine horse], disgusted at his impertinence, 'don't think that that embroidery of thine prevents our knowing thee to be an ass'.[8]

Not always elegant: a Grévy's zebra takes a roll in the dust.

The zebra is, then, at once exceptionally exotic and curiously common. Its form closely resembles that of a donkey or pony – whose presence in any city centre would attract little attention – but in place of a drab grey-brown coat, it offers something truly spectacular. Like the fictional unicorn, it is a magical variation on a familiar form, except the zebra not only exists, but may well have pre-dated the rest of the horse family. As David Willoughby has argued,

> the common interpretation of a zebra is that it is a striped horse, or a striped donkey. But it would probably be more accurate to regard horses and donkeys as zebras in which the stripes have been partially or completely lost.[9]

The so-called Hagerman horse (or American zebra), discovered in Hagerman, Idaho, in 1928, and thought to be about 3.5 million years old, is considered to have been closer in kind to a Grévy's zebra than to any modern horse – although skeletons cannot confirm that the animal was striped. The widely held belief that the earliest horse was, in fact, a zebra – and that zebras may have once roamed across North America – is nevertheless an intriguing one.[10] In this reading, zebras are not extraordinary horses; horses are extraordinary zebras.

It isn't just the stripes that differentiate the zebra from the rest of the horse family. As Pennant reminds us, the zebra is also notoriously 'untameable'. There are many people who would disagree with this statement, or read it as a challenge. As this book will prove, the dream of the domesticated zebra is a stubborn one, particularly among Western audiences. Encouraged by the biblical promise that nature was created largely for the benefit of man, non-African responses to the zebra have long been obsessed with the animal's practical value. The Italian explorer

Filippo Pigafetta (1533–1604), one of the first Europeans to write about the zebra, noted in 1591 that if zebras 'were made tame, they would serve to run and draw for the wars'. After all, as he wrote,

> Mother *Nature* seemeth to have sufficiently provided in every country for the commodity and necessity of man, with divers sorts of Creatures, of nourishments, and temperature of ayre, to the end he should want nothing.[11]

The idea that an animal should exist for some purpose other than to be useful to men seems not to have occurred to him, let alone subsequent explorers.

It is likely that people will never stop trying to tame zebras. Because they look like, and are closely related to, horses, humans have long been determined to treat them in the same way. The problem is that zebras, as a whole, have not proven amenable to domestication. There are exceptions – countless stories of tamed zebras, such as Zebedee, a young zebra purchased by a Dorset racehorse trainer in 2009 and ridden to the local pub (to the delight of tabloid newspapers).[12] Such stories – relatively common from the eighteenth century to the present day – prove little, however, beyond the fact that it is possible to train single zebras to accomplish basic tasks.[13] None of this does much to disturb the reality that the zebra's stylish look comes with a skittish temperament, less generously classed as truculence or hostility. Along with the fact that most zebras are simply too small to support a human passenger, this disposition – which proves handy when sharing a habitat with a lion – has ensured that, as Pennant memorably put it, they have proved largely 'useless' as far as the human race is concerned. Despite our best efforts, zebras have retained their wildness, refusing to comply with the popular

A distinctly brown zebra from a 19th-century European print published by Diedrich Carl Muller & Co.

fantasy of riding around on a black-and-white striped horse, or keeping herds of zebra in public parks. By running swiftly into the woods, by a hard kick of their powerful hind legs or by a stubborn bite (once they've sunk their teeth into something, zebras don't like to let go, as many a zookeeper has discovered), zebras have established their freedom again and again.

Pennant's long list of adjectives – 'elegant . . . gregarious, vicious, untameable, useless' – suggest an animal that humans have long struggled to define. Which one of these words best describes the zebra? Though zebras are everywhere in contemporary culture – from children's books to live-action films – the defining characteristics of a zebra are not easy to pinpoint. It could be argued that the zebra's popularity is closely related to its enduring strangeness, to its simultaneous closeness to something with which we are very familiar – the horse or donkey – and radical difference to anything else on the planet. As far as humans are concerned, the zebra is, as Pennant realized, a mass

le 25 — Mai 1904.

Postcard showing zebra-driving in Paris, 1904.

of contradictions: common and exotic, glamorous and ferocious, sociable and sullen.

The French writer Alexandre Jardin is one of several people to identify with the zebra, naming both his novel of 1988 (*Le Zèbre*) after the animal, as well as his subsequent organization, Bleu Blanc Zèbre, a collective which seeks to mobilize French citizens to solve social problems.[14] The power of the herd and the stubborn awkwardness of zebras seem to be the qualities that attract him. A peaceful herbivore that has nonetheless refused to give in to human expectations, the zebra is, as this book will show, an animal that has regularly excited outsiders. Due to the black-and-white dress forced on nineteenth-century convicts, it even has a criminal association. The mercurial zebra refuses to fit the mould, which is what makes its history so compelling. Zebras are, in a sense, the ultimate animal rebels. They have not only resisted domestication, but stymied generations of scientists eager to explain their extraordinary appearance. As Tim Caro, author of the most recent (and perhaps most wide-ranging) study of the subject has argued, 'the reason that zebras are striped is still enigmatic and captivating and constitutes one of the great mysteries of biology.'[15] Another zebra-specialist, Jonathan Kingdon, notes that 'even today, zebras remain aberrant animals in minds and vocabularies, engendering a popular folklore that has inhibited serious scientific investigation of an important phenomenon.'[16]

This book is an effort to trace that folklore, to look closely at how humans have represented zebras across the ages, and what this says, not just about zebras, but about ourselves. The description of the zebra as 'useless' tells us nothing about what it means to be a zebra, after all, but a lot about the way humans

Zebra stripes: still one of the great mysteries of biology.

traditionally approach animals. Because zebras are grumpy in the presence of humans, they are labelled as inherently grumpy animals. A zebra might contend, however, that any sensible animal would be cantankerous in the presence of humans, in light of the way humans have traditionally treated animals. We need to be mindful that animals are frequently viewed in relation to what they can do for us, or how they make us feel. Animals, in the end, are a human invention. They give us cues, which we weave into stories, frequently fantastical in nature. As all animals are, the zebra is as much a concept as a living creature.

The relationship between the defining characteristics of an animal, and the meanings that have been attached to it by different cultures, can be difficult to resolve – though in the case of the zebra, it is at least clear that its mysterious cultural persona is echoed in its consistently contentious natural history. The question of what constitutes a zebra in the biological sense – and what lies behind its recognizable features – is not, after all, a closed one. Zebras are as much a moving target scientifically as they are culturally.

As far as most people are concerned, a zebra is a black-and-white striped horse that lives in Africa. Popular as the animal is, little attention is given – as is the case with so many animals – to the variations within the subgenera. In the case of the zebra, these can be complex, not to mention controversial.[17] Zebras were categorized under a wide variety of names well into the twentieth century, and it is only recently that some consensus has been reached. In 1974 David Willoughby published a list of 'terms proposed or used for zebras of the Burchell's [that is, plains] species and the quagga' between 1788 and 1924.[18] It contained 35 names, the majority of which are now long forgotten.

The origin of the zebra probably lies, as with all equids, in North America – though since the end of the last ice age, they

A zonkey (zebra–donkey hybrid).

have been confined to the African continent. The point at which zebras deviated from ancestral horses – and why this happened – remains a matter of speculation, although it seems to have occurred about half a million years ago.[19] Research into skeletal, chromosomal and behavioural variations within extant equid species is very much ongoing, and continues to generate important questions concerning their evolutionary history.

Western science currently sorts zebras into three species, making up almost half of the seven existing equid species: the plains zebra (*Equus quagga*), the mountain zebra (*Equus zebra*) and Gréyy's zebra (*Equus greyyi*), within which a number of subspecies have been recognized.[20] The species have been known to appear in mixed herds, but are not thought to interbreed, although hybrids have existed in captivity. Interbreeding within Equidae in general is also known, with notable 'zebroids' including 'zonkeys' or 'zedonks' (a zebra–donkey hybrid), 'zebrules' (zebra–mule) and 'zetlands' (zebra–Shetland pony). Such hybrids are usually born sterile.

Within the three species, there are notable differences in appearance, habitat, behaviour and population size. As Willoughby observes, 'there are a great deal more structural (i.e. skeletal) differences between some forms of zebras than there are, for example, between a lion and a tiger.'[21] Beyond their distinctive patterning – within which there are, of course, not only group variations, but individual deviations – the subgenera nonetheless have the following general qualities in common.

First and foremost, zebras are social animals, commonly found in small family groups (roughly seven animals), which can form part of herds of a hundred or more. These groups consist of a stallion, a small group (or harem) of mares and their offspring.

Plains zebras grooming.

Grévy's zebras differ from plains and mountain zebras, which are nomadic by nature, in defending specific territories. Surplus stallions (that is, male zebras who have failed to attract a mare, or are yet to reach sexual maturity) often group together. Fights between stallions over mares are common, and can be violent. Following successful mating, zebras have a gestation period of about a year, depending on the subgenera. Connections between individual zebras have recently been described as 'loose and fluid', especially within the sexes.[22] The strongest bonds, unsurprisingly, are made between mothers and children, who regularly engage in the practice of 'skin-nibbling'.[23] Groups communicate with braying, barking calls and snorts. Hostility can be shown by

Zebra foal and mother.

A plains zebra herd, accompanied by a giraffe, wildebeest, oryx and ostrich.

'laying back their ears'.[24] Fleeing zebras make a distinct barking call that helps establish contact between family groups. This call – often written as 'kwa-ha' – is probably responsible for the naming of the quagga. Grévy's zebra calls are often described as more of a bray than a bark.

Zebras tend to have good relationships with fellow herbivores, especially wildebeests (although not in the case of mountain zebras), Thomson's gazelles, ostriches and occasionally giraffes. Their main predators – aside from humans – are lions, against which groups employ sentries, especially during night-time rest. Lions typically target the young, the old and the sick. Though zebras have a fierce kick, their main defence against the lion lies in the protection of the herd (that is, in not getting caught in the first place). Other key predators include hyenas, wild dogs, leopards and cheetahs – although these animals will usually only target young zebras. All zebras attract their fair share of insects, the significance of which, as Chapter Five reveals, has recently come to play a large part in the age-old question of why zebras have stripes in the first place.

Zebras are odd-toed ungulates, which means that, like horses, they have one large toe. They have high-crowned, durable teeth and powerful jaws designed for continuous grass-grazing, and large eyes with binocular vision, but no ability to bring objects into sharp focus. In the wild, they have a lifespan of 20–25 years, though zebras in captivity have been known to live for more than forty years. The answer to the long-running question as to whether zebras are white with black stripes, or black with white stripes is now widely thought to be the latter (though several sources continue to have it otherwise).[25]

The high international profile of the zebra might ensure that its safety is of greater concern than many lesser-known animals; nevertheless, it remains the case that two of the three species, as noted below, are currently listed as 'vulnerable' and 'endangered'. Zebra conservation is no less critical today than it has been at any time during the last century. The threats to zebras are wide-ranging, from over-exploitation and habitat destruction to climate change, and differ across subgenera. As migratory animals, zebras are especially affected by the presence of barriers such as the Red Line in Namibia, or the creation of new roads in Tanzania's Serengeti. Though the latter may bring more tourism to the region, and improve the lives of local populations, environmentalists worry that it will increase levels of roadkill.[26] While animals such as zebras are vital components of attracting tourism, containing and controlling animals whose health depends on freedom of movement remains a perpetual challenge.

All species of zebra have various alternative names given to them by African cultures. As these are manifold, and spellings differ, we have chosen to use only the standard Western names here.

The most common, varied and wide-ranging of the three zebra species is the plains zebra. Formerly known as 'Burchell's zebra' (after the British explorer William Burchell, whose name is now attached to a subspecies), the 'common zebra' or 'painted quagga', the plains zebra can be found as far north as Ethiopia, and as far south as northern South Africa. As of 2003, there are six accepted subspecies of plains zebra: the quagga (*Equus quagga quagga*, now extinct), Burchell's zebra (*Equus quagga burchelli*), Grant's zebra (*Equus quagga boehmi*), Chapman's zebra (*Equus quagga chapmanii*), Crawshay's zebra (*Equus quagga crawshayiii*) and the Maneless Zebra (*Equus quagga borensis*).[27] Some authorities still recognize Selous' zebra (*Equus quagga selousi*) as a subspecies, or list only five subspecies.[28] The stripe patterns of these subspecies differ greatly, from the profuse, narrow markings of Crawshay's, to the sparse, semi-striped quagga (thought for

Plains zebra (*Equus quagga*). Linocut by Samuel Shaw.

many years to have been a completely different species). Many plains zebras – especially Burchell's – have so-called 'shadow stripes', thin grey or brown stripes appearing between the bolder black. The almost endless variations in patterning go some way towards explaining why plains zebras have historically been divided into so many groups, as nineteenth-century naturalists struggled to impose order on a visually diverse ensemble. As a recent study has shown, however, 'cranially, [plains zebras] are all much alike.'[29]

Numbers of plains zebra in Africa are estimated at above 500,000, of which the largest number can be found in the Serengeti National Park in Tanzania (founded in 1951, with zebra conservation partly in mind). The geographical range of the plains zebra is considerably smaller than it used to be, with subspecies such as the quagga having been driven to extinction. The plains zebra is currently categorized as 'near threatened' on the International Union for Conservation of Nature (IUCN) list of threatened species.

Recent research published in *Oryx*, the International Journal of Conservation, suggests the migration of plains zebra 'ranks as the longest of all known mammal migrations in Africa'.[30] In 2012 researchers tagged and tracked eight female zebras as they made their annual journey from northeastern Namibia into Botswana and back again, a round trip that totalled more than 480 km (300 miles), and involved several thousand zebra. Such migrations were probably much more common than they are now; the reason why this one is still able to take place owes much to the existence of transboundary conservation areas such as KAZA (the Kavango–Zambezi Transfrontier Conservation Area), which allow zebras to move freely across national boundaries.

Mountain zebra
(*Equus zebra*).
Linocut by
Samuel Shaw.

Mountain zebra
(*Equus zebra*).
Linocut by
Samuel Shaw.

MOUNTAIN ZEBRA (*Equus zebra*)

Equus zebra currently consists of two subspecies, *Equus zebra zebra* (Cape mountain Zebra) and *Equus zebra hartmannae* (Hartmann's zebra). The former, as suggested by its name, can be found only in isolated areas of the Cape Province, most notably the Mountain Zebra National Park, founded in 1937 near the city of Cradock in the Eastern Cape. The latter are found mostly in Namibia and southwest Angola. Numbers of mountain zebras are estimated at around 9,000, on which basis they are currently listed as 'vulnerable'. Numbers of Cape mountain zebras are said to have crept as low as 100 in the 1930s to 1950s, but have shown promising signs of a revival in the last ten years. Their presence around the Cape ensured that they were the first type of zebra encountered by early visitors to southern Africa, and brought back to Europe. They were also the first species to be protected by law, although this did little to stave off their decline across the nineteenth century in particular. The conservation of the mountain zebra is complex: 'it is deemed a pest, competing with goats and cattle for food, breaking fences and causing erosion' and is still hunted 'both legally and illegally'. Since the mountain zebra 'lives in an arid environment with large variability in annual rainfall, some years are good for population growth but drought years are not'. [31] Conservationists can do their best to control fence construction, but there is little they can do about climate change.

The species' name refers, unsurprisingly, to the fact that mountain zebras are mostly found in mountainous areas. Mountain zebras have large hearts which allow them to live in high altitudes, and narrow hooves for moving across rugged terrain. They group in small harems: one male, three to five females and their foals. They are not territorial. They are water dependent, and feed on short, coarse grass. Mountain zebras are distinct from other zebras largely because of their smaller size, their tufted tail and their conspicuous dewlap (the loose flap of skin that hangs from their throats). The stripes of the mountain zebra tend to go all the way down the legs, but not across the belly. Hartmann's zebras are larger than Cape mountain zebras, with more widely spaced stripes.

GRÉVY'S ZEBRA (*Equus grevyi*)

This species – the largest and heaviest of the zebras, containing no subspecies – has traditionally been found in central and eastern Africa, though numbers have begun to fall rapidly over the last fifty years, with a decline of 50 per cent in the last two decades. They are now found only in small pockets of land in Ethiopia and Kenya. The total population is estimated at around 2,500, compared to more than 15,000 in the 1970s. Grévy's are now

Grévy's zebra (*Equus grevyi*). Linocut by Samuel Shaw.

classified by the IUCN as an 'endangered' species. Habitat loss and hunting (for skins, primarily, but occasionally for medicinal purposes) are thought to be the main causes of this decline.

Grévy's zebras get their name, in use since 1882, from the former French President Jules Grévy (1807–1891), courtesy of the French naturalist Émile Oustalet.[32] On account of their northeastern range, they were the first zebras to be introduced to Europe, where they went by the name Hippotigris.

As noted above, Grévy's do not maintain cohesive herds, but males defend small territories, although fights with possible rivals only occur when oestrous females are present. Territory boundaries are marked by middens (that is, dung piles). They are not as water dependent as plains or mountain zebras, and can go for three days without water if necessary. Grévy's are known especially for their thick necks, broad ears and narrow, even stripes. Grévy's zebras usually have white, stripe-less bellies. They have the longest gestation period (390 days) of any equid. Their lifespan is about twenty years. Grévy's can weigh up to 400 kg (880 lb).

The natural history of the zebra, as summarized above, is rich and complex – and continues to raise questions not just for scientists and environmentalists, but for society at large, as our understanding of what is distinct about the zebra continues to evolve. In the following pages, we trace the lively history of the zebra, in Africa and beyond, from its early appearance on ancient rock art and mosaics, to eighteenth-century pamphlets and Victorian hunting guides, culminating in paintings, advertisements and animations. We show how the zebra has come to mean many things to many people – a personal totem, a high-class commodity, the inevitable symbol for the letter 'Z' and the inspiration for a striped street-crossing – and continues to surprise us. Today the zebra might be consumed as an imported steak, purchased as an exotic pet or feature as an interior design statement. The monochrome stripes of the zebra – long debated by naturalists and scientists for their function – have, in recent times, been likened

Zebra barcode street art, maker unknown.

to a barcode and metaphorically invoked as a critique of consumerism and the loss of the individual. Celebrity zebras include Queen Charlotte's zebra (painted by George Stubbs in 1763), Seoul Zoo's 'Zelle', and 'Khumba', the fictional hero of a children's film and the name given to a foal born as part of the regenerative Quagga Project. This book will show how the zebra's history engages and intersects with diverse and rich topics, including eighteenth-century humour and consumerism, imperialism, surrealist art, and wartime dazzle painting.

1 Zebras at Home

The significance of the zebra to some African cultures is marked on the landscape itself. Primarily found in South Africa, Namibia and Botswana, rock art – the earliest examples of which are thought to be 20,000 to 28,000 years old – depicts a variety of animals and human figures. Zebras are not as common a feature of southern African rock art as antelope or eland; nevertheless, there are multiple instances in which they appear, each subject to a variety of interpretations.

The Limpopo basin has the largest concentration and number of animal figures depicted in South African rock art, dating back only a few centuries. For instance, Kaoxa's Shelter, a site in the Matshete hills, contains images of sixteen animal species across roughly two hundred different rock paintings. Kaoxa is the !Kung San's Lord of the Animals and rules over a spirit world full of creatures. The San people are hunter-gatherers who lived – and continue to live – in South Africa, Botswana and Namibia. There are about 95,000 San today, though only a few thousand are hunter-gatherers. Individual groups of San include the !Kung, IXam and Naro. In the eighteenth and nineteenth centuries, Dutch and later British colonial settlement led to the extermination and forced acculturation of San groups across southern Africa. In the twentieth century, too, San people have increasingly adopted agrarian lifestyles. However, through field research in

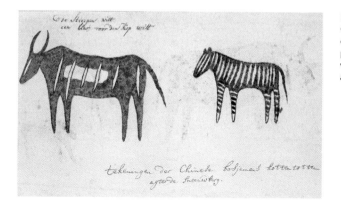

ethnography, anthropology and archaeology, the rock paintings have been contextualized as part of a San religious belief system and practices.

San beliefs about the zebra link them to water as well as to the supernatural potency that was given to them by the original San people, their ancestors. The IXam of the Northern Cape believed that the water spirits were striped like zebras. IXam women painted ochre stripes on young men to protect them from lightning. Other Kalahari San groups also associate the stripes of the zebra with lightening and rain. Indeed, the !Kung call heavy storm clouds /kewsi (zebra) because they move suddenly and downpour unexpectedly. The zebra (as seems to be the case in many African cultures) is also associated with feminine beauty, with !Kung girls decorating their thighs and cheekbones with ochre or ash in imitation of zebra stripes. Scarification marks can represent zebra stripes, too. Some !Kung women draw and tattoo zebra stripes on their buttocks, thighs and cheekbones. In the past, San zebra markings might have been even more extensive: in the 1860s San women in Namibia were reported to have painted black-and-white stripes on their entire bodies.[1]

San rock painting from the Drakensberg Mountains, South Africa. The painting seems to depict two therianthropes; men transforming into a zebra and antelope.

33

Elsewhere in Africa, zebra have inspired aesthetics and personal grooming in other ways. Men of tribes living to the south of Luanda, Angola, used to adopt a hairstyle called *pafu*, in which the hair was 'shaved at both sides above the ears, with a mane of hair running across the centre of the head, from nape to a pointed upsweep over the forehead, to resemble the zebra which they revered'. In the nineteenth century, Ngoni and Zulu headdresses used zebra manes tied around the head so that they stood in an imposing fan shape.[2]

The significance of the zebra to groups such as the San is further elucidated by the folk tale tradition. 'The Branding of the Animals', for instance, is a story passed on orally to remind San of the bonds between humans and animals. Unlike European visitors, African cultures have rarely, if ever, hunted zebra for sport. Eating zebra, however, has always been a part of the San experience, and when talking about the meat, tales that respect

Robert Jacob Gordon's depiction of San rock paintings, 1777, watercolour with artist's notes.

the animals are often told. The following telling of 'The Branding of the Animals' was recorded by the anthropologist Megan Biesele in the Kalahari in the early 1990s. Long ago, the original San were sitting around talking and decided to write the name of all the animals on their hides. People would no longer be people, but would have markings of different designs and would be animals. Names were given to each animal, and they were marked with *n/om* – a supernatural potency:

> The zebra came up and they drew stripes all over its body with the n/om (supernatural potency). Then they stepped back to look at the zebra's stripes. 'This is a pretty pattern here', they said. 'See how the n/om has marked lovely stripes on the zebra. Let's make stripes on ourselves to imitate him so we'll be beautiful too.' So they marked themselves with the n/om to look like the graceful zebra. Yes, long ago people imitated the stripes of the zebra on their own bodies.[3]

The zebra, then, was once human, and became a zebra by being marked by the ancestors of the San who, in turn, marked themselves to resemble the zebra.

Numerous African tales recount zebra-stripe narratives (a tradition that Western readers may be familiar with from the work of Rudyard Kipling, who deals with the zebra in his story 'How the Leopard Got his Spots', published in 1902). In one story from Lake Chad, a different account as to how the zebra got its stripes is offered. A zebra was caught stealing water from a well by a tortoise and tied to a tree to punish him for the theft. The tortoise planned to throw the thief into a fire, but he escaped and chose to run through the blaze. The zebra was seared and to this day carries the stripes that were seared into his skin.[4]

Another story from southern Africa, meanwhile, has it that a zebra was scorched by ashes kicked up from a fire made by a baboon. The baboon had greedily claimed a waterhole for his own use, an impertinence for which he was kicked onto rocks behind the waterhole by the zebra. The zebra kicked so hard that he staggered back into the fire. The baboon was forever changed, too, his red bare-bottom a reminder of being kicked by a zebra and landing on rocks.[5]

Zebra stripes continue to shape the animal's symbolic meaning across contemporary African culture. A Maasai proverb says that 'a man without culture is like a zebra without stripes.' The Maasai, a group of around a million pastoralists, have, in recent decades, been faced in Kenya and Tanzania with government policies to persuade or compel them to adopt a sedentary lifestyle. Maasai cultural practices have been threatened even as their cultural diversity has been packaged as an attractive image for tourism. For the Maasai, the idea that, as a people estranged from their roots and traditions, they might one day be like a zebra without stripes is not far-fetched.

This zebra proverb has migrated elsewhere across the continent, appearing on mural walls in Soweto and Lesedi Culture Village, South Africa, and posted online on social media throughout Africa and beyond. The proverb was also the title of a controversial documentary film from 2002 on the subject of the international adoption of South African babies. In the years following the film, the international adoption of South African babies and children by foreigners was limited to those who had been resident in South Africa for at least five years. So, too, was surrogacy limited to long-term or permanent residents, as South Africa sought to avoid the creation of a commercial surrogacy market fuelled by wealthy foreigners. This policy sought to prevent the creation of adoptees or surrogates without South African stripes.[6]

In 1980, John Berger wrote an influential essay titled 'Why Look at Animals?', in which he argued that it is difficult to see real animals – even when they are right in front of us – precisely because they are marginalized. In zoos, animals like the zebra are a 'living monument to their own disappearance'.[7] This disappearance is literal and metaphorical. We are surrounded by representations of zebras and enamoured with their image. And yet the sight of a zebra, whether in the zoo or the wild, can be elusive, disappointing or frustrating.

The long and intimate relationship that African cultures have shared with the zebra, along with the whole structure of their belief systems, is, like the wild zebra itself, also under threat. The multiple meanings that zebras have held for different peoples, over different times, must not be forgotten. Culture, like the zebra, needs its stripes.

The Shona, a Bantu group of some 10 million people in Zimbabwe and neighbouring countries, use *mitupo*, or totems, as markers of identity and lineage – a tradition stretching back to the Shona dynasties of the eleventh century and beyond. Totem animals include the eland, buffalo, lion and monkey. Totems are passed on through the lineage of the father, with sexual relations between members of the same totem being forbidden. As a cultural practice, then, the totem is a marker of ancestral bloodline and exogamy – marrying outside of one's clan. Taboos prohibited the animal totem from being hunted or consumed; human and animal sharing a sense of spirit – or *mweya* – that binds them together. Those of the zebra totem did not hunt, kill or consume zebra.

Shona praise poetry celebrates the attributes of totem animals, ancestors and clan members. One zebra praise poem thanks the zebra, 'iridescent and glittering creature', for its beauty and peaceful nature. It is also kin, an animal with a 'lineage that stretches everywhere, owners of the land'.[8] A member of the zebra (*mbizi*, *madube* or *tembo*) totem told an anthropologist in 1933 that 'the zebra has got our manners; we have the same way of living.' A friend of the American anthropologist H. P. Junod killed a zebra in the presence of Office Muhlanga, a man of the zebra totem, who was visibly moved by the death of his totem and 'began a whole funeral oration' for the animal.[9] Meanwhile, Shona burials from Mapungubwe, an eleventh- and twelfth-century city south of Great Zimbabwe, have revealed that totems played a role in guiding the deceased to the afterlife. A figurine of clay moulded into the shape of an animal totem, like a zebra, was sometimes interred with the bodies of the deceased. Zebra marks of black and white also appear on the walls of stone structures at Great Zimbabwe, a hill city occupied between the eleventh and fifteenth centuries. A soapstone bowl fragment in the South African Museum, dated to the same period, depicts a zebra in procession with a dog, bird and baboon. In Shona praise poetry, the zebra's stripes are represented as an intertwining pattern resembling the joining of male and female elements; at Great Zimbabwe painted zebra stripes appear on the walls of a structure thought to be a premarital school, a *domba*, for the initiation of women into adulthood. Such stripes have also been found on pots.[10] The Zimbabwean name Madhuve means 'woman/women of the zebra totem' and is still a name given to girls in Zimbabwe as a proper name. Those with female relatives who are of the zebra totem may affectionately call them *Manjenjenje*. These women are said to be especially beautiful and graceful – like the zebra. In 2014, a Zimbabwean newspaper, *The Herald*, reported that a man 'has taken the love for Manjenjenje to another level by going for the real thing: domesticating a zebra'. A single 65-year-old cattle farmer, Simon Temba, first met the zebra at 5 a.m. when she turned up outside the door of his farm. She was small and slept with the calves on his farm. Temba called her Judy or Madhuve, and he told *The Herald* that she is his 'long lost sister' – his totem sent by his ancestors. Judy grazes with Temba's cattle by the road-side, where she attracts the attention of motorists: 'she knows that she is beautiful and sometimes enjoys walking a distance from the cattle so that people admire her.' *The Herald* reported that although Temba 'loves and cherishes the animal' and that 'her stripes make him happy', his zebra totem has attracted criti-cism from his neighbours; some neighbours have accused him of *juju* – witchcraft – or regard him as 'crazy'.[11]

Another contemporary news story from Zimbabwe reflects a different kind of zebra scandal. A Zanu PF politician called Dorothy Mabika was charged with the theft of stock and obstruct-ing the course of justice after she took dairy calves into her possession in 2012, on behalf of Zanu PF. She allegedly did not hand over the animals to the party and instead altered documents to conceal the crime. Mabika stated that the Minister of State

Great Zimbabwe.

Affairs, Didymus Mutasa, had a vendetta against her because she turned down his sexual advances, and it was he who framed her. Mabika's totem is the zebra, and Mutasa's totem is the buffalo. Mabika's lawyer reported that Mutasa had said 'A zebra and buffalo can graze together, but if the zebra refuses to graze with the buffalo, the buffalo will gore the zebra.' Zimbabwean newspapers reported this totemic wordplay as a thinly veiled threat to destroy Mabika's political career. She was later acquitted in 2013 on the grounds that there was no evidence of theft.[12]

Zimbabweans are not the only Africans to have animal totems – peoples in Uganda and the Democratic Republic of Congo also practise this cultural tradition. However, with Zimbabwe, the loss of totems is an issue with far-reaching societal consequences. Robert Mugabe and other Zimbabwean politicians have, in the past, scorned the descendants of foreign nationals as *miwidi* – 'totemless elements of alien origin' – and withheld from them the right to vote (a right that was later constitutionally reinstated).[13] Cities, in particular, are suspiciously viewed as places where people become totem-less; immigrants from neighbouring Zambia and Mozambique are 'totem-less', and, in particular, when foreign men marry Zimbabwean women, their children will be totem-less too. The international marriages of the Zimbabwean diaspora also, in some circumstances, produce 'totem-less' children. Mary J. Maher, a Zimbabwean married to an Irish man and resident in the United Kingdom, reflects on the loss of totem-culture:

I sometimes feel sad I have destroyed my culture. For example, my family's totem is zebra and my older children's totem is lion, but my younger children have no totem because that is passed on through the father, and my husband's culture does not believe in totems . . . So all Zimbabwean women who marry outside their totem-carrying culture kill off this tradition, while the Zimbabwean men pass it onto their children.[14]

Zebras mark national identity in modern Africa in different ways, too. The coat of arms of Botswana features two zebras: one holding an ear of sorghum, the other an ivory tusk. Postage stamps from African countries – both colonial and post-independence – have regularly featured zebras.

South African Stamp, 1961.

This chapter has dwelt on race, belonging and identity in Africa. The stripes of the zebra have also been used as a way of thinking about race, about 'blackness' and 'whiteness', in different contexts. Earlier, in his book *Black Skins White Mask* (1967), Franz Fanon called a desire to be acknowledged not as black but white as a 'zebra striping of the mind'.[15] His book was an analysis of the negative psychological effects of racism and the cultural aliena-tion of colonialism. Fanon, born in Martinique and educated in France in medicine and psychiatry, argued that discourses of 'whiteness' caused some blacks to reject their 'blackness': 'out of the blackest part of my soul, across the zebra striping of my mind, surges this desire to be suddenly white.' However, black Ameri-cans and Canadians have also used the zebra as a metaphor for race and the politics surrounding it. In his essay 'Zebra: Growing Up Black and White in Canada' (1994, republished 2001), Law-rence Hill wrote about his experience as the 'light-skinned son of a Black man and white woman'. His father

occasionally called me a zebra, which I thought was quite funny. Within our family, it became a private expression for people of mixed race. . . . 'Zebra', of course, sounds faintly ridiculous. I wouldn't use it in a serious conversation, but I prefer it to 'mulatto'.[16]

The Republic of Botswana's coat of arms.

Mercedes Baines's poem 'Half Baked Zebra Cake' (1997) explores her self-identity as a mixed-race black, underscoring it with humour to reject notions of 'half-breed' and 'mulatto' (a zebra cake is a chocolate and vanilla marbled sponge cake):

> There's a restaurant that sells Zebra Cake
> It's a personal favorite
> . . .
> I eat it as a metaphor for devouring myself.
> . . .
> I know waiters don't get the joke
> Perhaps it's really not that funny
> As I eat my own derogatory definition with a smile and a
> chocolate rush.[17]

Barack Obama, the 44th President of the United States, and the nation's first black president, has often attracted commentaries on race. His 'blackness' – or indeed 'whiteness' – has drawn interest from across the political spectrum. In 2014, Jim Thompson, the chairman of the Winnebago County Republican Central Committee, described Obama as 'the offspring of a donkey and a zebra, black and white legs, rest all donkey . . . part white part black and all a**'. Thompson later apologized for his 'joke'.[18]

During an interview on NBC's *Today* show, the American comedian Chris Rock spoke about his role as the voice of the zebra character Marty in *Madagascar 3*. Rock said that he had decided to take on the role 'in honour of our zebra president, black and white, white and black'. Rock added, 'I love our president, you know, but he's black and white, he appeals to all . . . we ignore the president's whiteness, but it's there, it's there.'[19] In the first movie of the successful franchise (*Madagascar*, 2005) Marty longs to return to Africa and to resolve his own sort of identity crisis: 'I'm ten years old. My life is half over and I don't even know if I'm black with white stripes or white with black stripes!' Alex the Lion later counts Marty's stripes and provides him with an answer: 'Hmm, 30 black and only 29 white, looks like you're black with white stripes after all. Dilemma solved.' David Gillota has written on Marty the Zebra's 'blackness' and argues that Marty is given a 'black identity' through Chris Rock's voice and a narrative that seeks a return to Africa.[20] As a case in point, in *Madagascar: Escape 2 Africa* (2008), upon arriving on the African mainland, Marty exclaims 'Our ancestral crib. It's in our blood. I can feel it . . . it's like *Roots*!'[21]

2 Zebras on the Move

> One might say that the painter of fate, with a strange brush,
> had left it on the page of the world.
> Nuruddin Muhammad Jahangir, Mughal Emperor, 1621[1]

This chapter traces the movements of the zebra through different
human cultures, from antiquity to the Enlightenment, observing
the zebra's passage – by both land and sea – along the crossroads
of empires.

The zebra does not appear – or, as the case might be, survive
– in the extant material and textual culture of the ancient Egyptians.[2] The conspicuous absence of this very conspicuous animal
is perhaps surprising in an African culture with extensive trade
networks that stretched down the Nile into Nubia (Sudan) and
beyond. This might be explained by the historical range of the
zebra; the zebra had long ceased to be an endemic species in
Egypt prior to the Predynastic period. This notwithstanding, the
range of the zebra extended to the very peripheries of the ancient
Egyptian world; Grévy's and plains zebra lived as far north as
Ethiopia and the Sudan. The ancient Egyptian elite did keep menageries, and living animals were often brought back by trading
expeditions. The tribute extracted from neighbouring lands regularly took the form of exotic animals: giraffes, elephants, leopards,
monkeys, baboons and gazelles were, for example, brought from
Nubia and the Land of Punt (eastern Ethiopia, Somalia and Eritrea) along with ebony, gold, ivory and myrrh. Might a zebra have
also been rendered as tribute to a pharaoh or bartered for by an
Egyptian trade delegation? It is probable that the zebra was, at

some point, known to or seen by at least some Egyptians, but it did not seemingly attain any special significance or attract lasting special interest; thus the monochrome stripes of the zebra do not grace the plastered walls of tombs or sheets of papyrus.

Although we cannot know whether a zebra became the property of an Egyptian pharaoh of the Old or New Kingdom, zebras were certainly present in Ptolemaic Egypt. The Greeks knew the zebra as the *hippotigris*, the striped horse – though ónagros, or wild ass, could also refer to a zebra. The coronation procession of Philadelphus, the second Ptolemaic king of Egypt, through Alexandria in 285 BC was a spectacular affair. Statues of deities and mythological figures were followed by portable altars and their attendants. Next, according to the writer Athenaeus, came the king's menagerie: 24 chariots drawn by four elephants each, twelve chariots drawn by antelopes, eight by pairs of ostriches and eight by zebras – in addition to lions, camels and buffaloes. In his *Library of History*, Diodorus Siculus, writing between the years 60 and 30 BC, noted that Philadelphus' menagerie brought to the attention of Greeks 'animals which had never before been seen and were objects of amazement'.[3]

Away from Alexandria, in the Ptolemaic Kingdom at Marisa – now Tel Maresha in modern Israel – what might be a zebra was painted onto the walls of a mountain tomb in around 200 BC. In addition to human figures in Greek dress and a hunting scene, there are depictions of an elephant, giraffe, rhinoceros, lion, porcupine and zebra, among others. These animals are painted alongside their names in Greek. Though the zebra is described as a 'wild ass' (ónagros), its very striking stripes and patterning have been identified as more fitting of a striped equid.[4] Marisa, a city in the foothills of the Judaean mountains, had a large Greek-speaking population. The tomb paintings suggest an interest in exotic animals across the Hellenistic world as objects of amazement and of the imagination. The zebra, or 'wild ass', and other exotic animals were painted alongside the griffin, an animal that had not been seen by anybody, but was thought to live in the East. The artist might have never seen a zebra or a wild ass in person, although it remains a possibility that they – or their patrons – did; after all, exotic animals were treading the roads of the empire on their way to Alexandria. If not, it is likely that zebras were circulating in the form of written descriptions or images.[5]

The zebra was also on the move throughout the Roman Empire, and on a much larger scale than in previous periods. The *spectacula*, or amphitheatre, had an important political and social role in Roman civil life. The *venationes*, or animal hunts, required mass mobilization of trained gladiators, captives or criminals – as well as the supply of wild animals. In these hunts, animals would be paraded and then either pitted against animal or human combatants. Trained animal hunters or soldiers were tasked with sourcing animals from across the empire and beyond. Alexandria, the city where Ptolemy II's zebra had drawn chariots, became a major city through which African animals were brought to Italy for the *spectacula*. The Roman historian Dio Cassius, in his *Roman History*, wrote of the lengths to which Plautian, the praetorian prefect (commander of the guard) to the emperor Septimius Severus (AD 193–211), went to acquire some zebra. Plautian ordered his centurions to steal zebras from islands in the Red Sea. As zebras were not found naturally on Red Sea islands, these had probably been stolen while en route to Persia, perhaps intended for the menageries of some of the Parthian kings.[6]

In the games of Severus' son, Emperor Caracalla (r. AD 198–217), zebras were trained to pull chariots; in 212, a zebra was also slain in the arena as part of a *venatio*. These zebras were probably those that had been captured by Plautian. Other accounts, perhaps exaggerated, write of ten or even twenty zebras appearing on a single occasion in games; for instance, ten zebras were said to have appeared in AD 248 during games that were held to celebrate the 1,000th anniversary of the foundation of Rome.[7]

Evidence for the spectacle of zebras – or at least, knowledge about the zebra – throughout the Levant in the late and post-Roman world is found in the form of mosaics dating from the sixth century. At Şanliurfia (known to the Byzantines as Justin-opolis), in southeastern Turkey, an extensive villa thought to be the residence of a Byzantine official was discovered in 2007. It contains a mosaic which depicts a man leading a zebra. In Gaza, Palestine, a zebra and a giraffe feature on the mosaic floor of a sixth-century synagogue. The sixth-century early Christian mon-astery at Beth She'an, Israel, also shows a zebra and giraffe, in addition to an elephant. This flurry of mosaic zebra depictions is joined, too, by the mosaic of a zebra being led by a boy in the sixth-century basilica at Mount Nebo, Jordan.[8] The depictions of exotic animals in Byzantine mosaics are thought not only to have been the products of pattern books and artistic imagin-ation. Gaza, for example, was at the juncture of caravan routes and thus a commercial centre; exotic animals might well have been traded and observed extensively here. Timotheus of Gaza tells us, for example, that in 496 an elephant and two giraffes were brought through Gaza from Ethiopia on the way to Emperor Anastasius; perhaps a zebra also found itself on the road to Constantinople.[9] Some historians, too, point to the naturalistic portrayal of the mosaic animals, suggesting that they were drawn from life rather than a pattern book. In both Christian and Jewish contexts, the zebra appears in several sixth-century mosaics across the Byzantine Empire; this suggests that the zebra held quite some interest to contemporaries – it was an animal gazed upon in life or heard of through the tales of travellers.

A zebra brought to the court of the Ming Emperor Yongle (r. 1402–24) from East Africa by the fleet of Admiral Zheng He (1371–1435).

福鹿

Sixth-century Byzantines, drawing upon a long Latin and Greek cultural heritage, had long been aware of the zebra; in contrast, the Chinese encountered the zebra for the very first time in thirteenth-century China. The fleets of Admiral Zheng He, sent out from China between 1405 and 1433, during the reigns of two emperors, were intended to be a manifestation of Chinese power; in addition to providing the benefits of up-to-date cartography and the opening up of diplomatic and trade relationships with distant lands, the voyages of the 'treasure fleets' were intended to signal the presence and authority of China as a naval and cultural force. Ships laden with porcelain, silks and other gifts commissioned by the imperial court returned with the productions of foreign lands – including 'rare birds and animals'. One of these animals was known as the *fu-lu*, or zebra (also called *hua-lu-fu*). The modern Chinese word for zebra is *bān mǎ* (斑马 – striped horse), but it is thought that the older Chinese word for the zebra – *fu-lu* – is derived from the Somali word for zebra, *fár'o*, the sound of which has the happy fortuity of carrying (with a little mispronunciation) the meanings of 'good fortune and happiness', or 'deer of good fortune' in Chinese. In 1417, a zebra was given to the Chinese as a gift in Mogadishu, Somalia, and this zebra was later presented to the Emperor Yong-Le. A few years later, in 1421, Zheng He purchased giraffes, zebras, cheetahs and lions so that he 'might take home creatures which other countries have not obtained'.[10] One Chinese writer described the zebra as 'like a donkey but with lovely variegated stripes', and this zebra was depicted – probably for the first time in Chinese culture – in the work *Pictures of the Birds and Beasts of Strange Lands*. The Emperor received these animals as tribute at the Feng-tian Gate, the gate at the edge of the complex in which important court audiences and state affairs were conducted in the Forbidden City. Ministers, apparently, gathered to congratulate the emperor, but his official response to these birds and beasts of strange lands was somewhat understated:

> It is not that I have any love for creatures from distant lands, but I think of the extreme sincerity with which these persons are come so far, and so my reception of them is no matter of congratulation.

No matter how lovely the deer of good fortune might have been, the value of the *fu-lu*, at least from the emperor's perspective, was in the power relations that this animal made visible – relationships of sincerity and fealty.[11]

The beaches of Eastern Africa yield broken fragments of pottery and porcelain that attest to a long history of contact across the Indian Ocean, dating from around the first millennium onwards. The green-hued celadon sherds scattered among sand and pebbles are the broken and discarded fragments of Chinese wares that were created – or rather, mass-produced – for luxury markets in India, the Middle East and Africa.[12] The coastal cities of Ethiopia and Somalia were connected to India and East Asia

English Chinoiserie-style 'Zebra' pearlware plate manufactured by Rogers, *c.* 1820s.

not only through intermediaries like Arab traders, but directly through their own envoys and merchants. In 1673, Emperor Yohannes I of Ethiopia sent his envoy, an Armenian called Murad, with a letter written in Arabic to the governor of the Dutch East India Company, Jan Maetzuyker. The letter informed the governor that he was being sent two animals that were 'so beautiful that no painter can depict them'.[13] The zebras, or 'striped asses of the woods', travelled with Murad to the coastal city of Mocha, Yemen, and then on to the city of Surat, India, on board an Indian trading vessel. In September 1674, the two zebras were on the move again, travelling on board a Moorish ship to Malacca, Malaysia. Here, the zebras were taken into the care of a representative of the Dutch East India Company. In February 1675, the zebras arrived in Batavia, present-day Jakarta, and finally reached their intended recipient. The zebras were kept in the garden of the governor's palace, and crowds gathered to see them. This was not, however, the end of the zebras' arduous journey;

they were to be re-gifted, as it were, and sent on to Japan. After the introduction of *sakoku*, Japan's national isolation or closed-door policy, in the early seventeenth century, the Dutch were the sole European nation granted permission to trade with Japan, and even then were restricted to a single trading concession. On a regular basis, the Dutch were obliged to form a tributary mission or embassy and were escorted to the court of the Tokugawa Shogun in Edo (present-day Tokyo). Here the Shogun received annual tribute in the form of European scientific instruments, mirrors, clocks, guns and rare animals. Thus, the zebras that had been given to the Dutch East India Company as a diplomatic gift became, in turn, Dutch tribute to the Japanese Shogun. In return, the Shogun gave 10,000 silver taels (one tael equalled forty grams of silver), along with 'thirty Japanese dresses', presumably silk garments of some sort.[14] The tributary embassy on the road usually turned heads because the 'red-haired' Dutch were a peculiar sight; the pair of zebras must also have given those Japanese that crowded to catch a glimpse of the foreign embassy cause for a second glance as they walked towards Edo.

Zebras from Ethiopia, later Abyssinia, circulated widely as tribute. Although two reached as far as Indonesia, and then ultimately Japan, a larger number of zebras was exchanged within the Islamic world as prudent diplomatic manoeuvres. Diplomatic letters accompanied by expensive goods such as silks, perfumes, oils and ceramics, as well as exotic animals, constituted an important part of diplomatic practice.

A survey of the diplomatic letters exchanged between the Islamic Mamluk sultans and their neighbours from the twelfth century onwards reveals an early tradition of the bestowal of zebras as favours. The Mamluk Sultanate stretched from Eritrea to Egypt and across the Levant. A letter from a Mamluk sultan to al-Mujahid Ali, Sultan of Yemen, thanked him profusely for his gift of a zebra, giraffe, elephant and tiger – sent along with expensive perfumes. The court of al-Nasir Muhammad received an embassy from Yemen in 1304 that included a zebra, elephant and giraffe clothed in gold-brocaded silk – in addition to costly Chinese jades and porcelain.[15] Sultan al-Zahir Baybars, ruler of Egypt and Syria, was well known in Christendom as a man who had captured crusader lands, and yet, in 1261, he (or perhaps his immediate predecessor, al-Malek, 'Alvandexaver') sent an embassy to the court of Alfonso x of Castile in Seville. Gifts sent to Alfonso x included opulent textiles and expensive jewels, as well as a giraffe, an elephant and 'an ass that was striped with one band white and the other black'.[16] Alfonso's exotic animals, including the zebra, are depicted in a manuscript known as the *Cantigas de Santa María*, a work that contains the miracles of 'Our Lady', with poems and songs extolling her virtues and deeds. In *Cantiga 29*, the zebra and other animals are depicted humbling themselves and kneeling before the Holy Virgin, 'as God wills that all creatures honour His Mother'. According to lore, the skins of these animals were displayed on the walls of Seville Cathedral. This may not be as far-fetched as it sounds; after all, Alfonso's crocodile was stuffed and hung from the ceiling of a cloister in the cathedral (a wooden replacement can be seen there today).[17]

Alfonso's zebra was very certainly absorbed into Christendom – a supplicant at the knees of the Virgin and, so legend goes, strung up in death on the walls of a cathedral. His zebra was part of a historical moment in the thirteenth century, an Islamic sultan courting a Christian king while simultaneously campaigning successfully against the crusader lands (Constantinople itself would be captured two centuries later). For contemporaries in Christendom, the later capture of Constantinople was met with fear and disbelief. A zebra had been present at that moment, too:

an animal that had probably originated in Ethiopia and came to the city as a present for Constantine XI. After the capture of Constantinople, thereafter Istanbul, in 1453, Mehmet II sent an embassy to Cairo to announce his victory. Captured Byzantine officials, two elephants and a zebra joined crates of silks, furs and other textiles as part of the triumphal parade; cheering crowds in the streets of Cairo greeted the parade of plundered booty.[18]

Much later, Ottoman rulers received a number of zebras from Ethiopia in the seventeenth century; on one occasion, in 1624, the gift of a zebra was intended to 'smooth over' the arrival of some Ethiopian Christian missionaries in the Red Sea area surrounding Massawa, a city on the coast of Eritrea; this zebra was then passed on to Istanbul.[19] Ludolphus' *Historia aethiopica* (1681) records that the emperor of Ethiopia sent three zebras to Istanbul on one single occasion.

Ethiopian zebras have an especially long history of walking along the crossroads of culture and civilizations; the zebra painted by Ustad Mansur at the Mughal Court in 1621, one of the finest representations of a zebra ever made, speaks of a keen interest in natural history in the Islamic world. The Mughal Empire, comprised of Hindustan and parts of Afghanistan, was a multicultural empire with a Muslim ruling class and Hindu or Sikh subjects. During the early 1620s, when a zebra came to the Mughal Court, the court was a powerful, opulent political and cultural force. Emperor Jahangir's court attracted artists, intellectuals and foreign dignitaries. The emperor was particularly interested in

Zebra by Ustad Mansur of the school of Jahangir, India, 1620–21, watercolour.

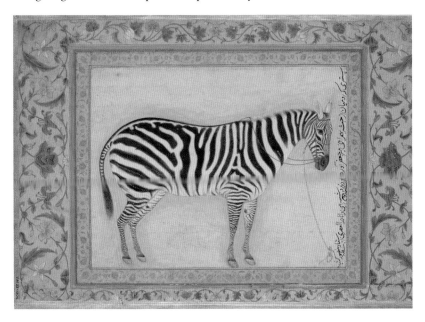

natural history and maintained a large menagerie and aviary, stocked with cheetahs, elephants and exotic birds (including a dodo). Ustad Mansur, an artist in the court's painting atelier, was commissioned by Jahangir to paint animals, birds and flowers. Jahangir was not only interested in depicting the animals as species; he desired 'portraits' that captured the peculiarities and individual characteristics of their subjects. In the sixteenth year of his reign, Jahangir was presented with a zebra by Mir Jafar, the governor of Surat and Cambay; this zebra had been brought by some Turks from Abyssinia. Jahangir's memoirs contain his first impressions of the zebra:

> I saw a wild ass, exceedingly strange in appearance, exactly like a lion [tiger]. From the tip of the nose to the end of the tail, and from the point of the ears to the top of the hoof, black markings, large or small, suitable to their position were seen on it. Round the eyes there was an exceedingly fine black line. One might say that the painter of fate, with a strange brush, had left it on the page of the world. As it was strange, some people imagined that it had been coloured. After minute enquiry into the truth, it became known that the Lord of the World was the Creator thereof.[20]

The black markings and lines of the zebra, left on the page of the world by the painter of fate, were in turn depicted by Jahangir's painter. Mansur's zebra wears a red bridle and is pictured staked to the bare ground. The plain foreground draws extra attention to the monochrome markings of the zebra. The image is bordered by a riot of colourful flowers and an inscription in Jahangir's own hand – a note on the provenance of the zebra and painting. This particular zebra did not, however, live for long at the Mughal court; it was sent as a royal gift to Persia to Shah Abbas.[21]

In the seventeenth century, with the exception of those like François Bernier who lived and travelled extensively outside of Europe, few Europeans had seen a living zebra. This is not to say that the zebra did not have a place in European natural history – although the English clergyman Edward Topsell did leave the zebra out of his *History of Four-footed Beasts* (1658), an odd omission since his work was based on Conrad Gessner's earlier work, *Historia animalium* (History of Animals, 1551), in which the zebra does appear. The *Zebra indica* was depicted, also, in Ulisse Aldrovandi's posthumous *De quadrupedibus soldipedibus* (The Four-footed Beasts Without Cloven Hooves, 1616).

Filippo Pigafetta's *Relatione del reame di Congo* (A Report of the Kingdom of the Congo, 1591) was a narrative account of the Portuguese trader Duarte Lopes's travels to the Congo and Angola, later translated into English, French and German. Lopes had set off for the Congo in 1578 to search for silver mines, and became an ambassador for Álvaro II Nimi a Nkanga, king of Congo, to King Phillip II and the Pope. Lopes was to report his findings to Pigafetta for compilation, but his accounts were thought, even at the time, to be fabulous. As noted in the introduction, Pigafetta was one of the first commentators to address the zebra's 'usefulness' via domestication, envisaging its future as a form of transport or war horse. However, the people of the Congo were obliged to 'employ men instead of beasts of burden' since they knew not 'how to tame zebras with bridle and saddle' (Europeans, it is implied, clearly knew better).[22] The accompanying illustration, an illustration that was adapted and diffused throughout Europe, depicted a zebra in a distinctly equine pose, prancing in a wooded, mountainous landscape. A coloured woodblock print of this image produced in Frankfurt in 1597 added a large walled and turreted city to the landscape, as well as dazzling yellow, white and black stripes to the zebra.

The Dutch settlements of the Dutch Cape Colony were, by the eighteenth century, a source of both knowledge about zebras and a market for shipping zebras to Europe. The colony had been established in 1652 and later became a concern of the Dutch East India Company. Thus, at the time that the Dutch presented the Abyssinian zebra to the Shogun of Japan, zebras – albeit different species of zebra – were fairly well known to them. Quaggas were exhibited at The Hague in the late 1740s, brought from the Cape. A quagga – the first zebra to reach British shores – was also kept at Kew by the Prince of Wales in the 1750s. This female quagga was brought from the Cape of Good Hope with a male – presumably another species of zebra – and drawn by George Edwards, a naturalist and librarian at the Royal College of Surgeons. It appeared in his *Gleanings of Natural History* (1758), where it was mistaken for a female zebra, an error which subsequent travellers repeatedly mocked.

In the eighteenth century, natural history was both a fashionable pastime and an Enlightenment intellectual pursuit. Most European readers encountered natural history in the pages of Georges-Louis Leclerc, Comte de Buffon's encyclopedic *Histoire naturelle* (1749–89), either in French or in translation. His entry on the zebra began on a much-repeated note of high praise: 'the zebra is perhaps the handsomest and most elegant of all quadrupeds.' Buffon noted that attempts to tame the zebra had hitherto ended in vain, basing his assessment on the male zebra in the royal menagerie in 1761. This zebra was 'very wild' when he arrived at the menagerie at Versailles; nevertheless, he had been 'brought to let a man sit on a saddle' on his back. This was only a partial success, however, as 'two men are obliged to hold the bridle while the third is on his back'. The zebra's character was described in distinctly unflattering terms: 'he is restive, like a vicious horse, and obstinate as a mule' – not a promising candidate for breaking in![23]

Unlike the journeys of many of the zebras in this chapter, the voyage of a zebra that arrived at Versailles in 1786 is well documented. The letters exchanged on the matter of a zebra for the king of France's menagerie provide an intriguing glimpse into the not inconsiderable challenge of bringing a zebra from the plains of the Cape to the Île-de-France. Historian Louise Robbins has documented this hunt for a zebra and called it 'The Zebra Quest'; it was a quest that required diplomacy, the calling in of favours and a great deal of luck.[24] The 1780s was a period of economic trouble for France, and the king was himself aware of the symbolic potential of the royal menagerie; indeed, he was painfully aware that the menagerie was in a sorry state, so he asked the duc de Noailles, prince de Poix – in his capacity as governor of Versailles – to acquire new animals for the menagerie. Thus, a chain of correspondence leading down from the highest echelons of the French state began. In January 1783, the prince de Poix wrote to the navy minister, the maréchal de Castries, to inform him that 'his majesty has decided that the menagerie will be maintained

Le Cheval rayé from *Les Anciennes Indes Series*, c. 1690–1730. A French tapestry created by the Gobelins manufactory, Paris.

Zebra indica depicted in John Jonston's *Historiae naturalis de quadrupetibus* (1655).

as a manifestation of royal magnificence . . . I am attaching a list of what has been requested; you will do me great pleasure to give the necessary orders'. This list included '2 zebras, male and female'. The navy minister passed an order along to the vicomte de Souillac, a high-ranking government official: 'Please take advantage of favorable occasions to entrust several reliable people to buy these animals. Nothing is to be neglected in fulfilling the prince de Poix's wishes.' The letter closed with an appeal to pecuniary restraint: 'Please send me the list of expenses incurred by these commissions. I urge you to take the most economic measures in this regard.' In early 1784 a French agent named Percheron in Cape Town received a letter from Souillac requesting two zebras. His response to Souillac was not promising: the people who lived near the mountains did not catch a zebra, despite being paid to do so. However, the governor of Cape Town had a zebra in his menagerie, and he would try to acquire that one.

George Edwards, 'The Female Zebra', etching from *Gleanings of Natural History* (1758). This animal was the first zebra to reach British shores. Though identified by Edwards as a female zebra, it was in fact a quagga.

ZEBRA femina, sive Mula sylvestris Africana. Drawn from the living Animal belonging to his Royal Highness the Prince of Wales.

60

Zebra Indica
Indianisch Maulthier.

Tab: V.

Equus Indicus
Indianisch Pferd.

Equus Hirsutus
Rauh Pferd.

In this Percheron was successful, and he arranged to have the animal shipped to France. This was easier said than done, as French captains refused passage to the animal, leading Percheron to engage the services of a private merchant ship. He wrote to the navy minister that a zebra was on the way with sufficient hay and wheat for the long journey. Unfortunately, unknown to both Percheron and the minister, the zebra died three days into the voyage and arrived dead in France. The zebra had been shipped along with a 'wild horse with zebra like stripes', but even this arrived in poor condition. After receiving a curt letter from the minister, Percheron replied that it was almost certainly the neglectful captain's fault that the zebra had died. After all, he had kept the animal for a year in a stable, and it had been in excellent shape when loaded on the ship. Months passed, and with a change of governance in the Cape came a more favourable situation for Percheron. The new governor was more amenable to assisting the French and gave orders across a territory of some 800 km (500 miles) for zebras. Finally, in November 1785, Percheron was successful and wrote to the navy minister to tell him that he had acquired two zebras and would ship them to France. He also told the minister that the debt of 120 piasters (the two zebras were worth about £300 pounds in English money in 1785, around £400,000 today) was owed, as the governor had paid for the zebra to be captured and maintained at the menagerie of the Dutch East India Company. Only a male set off for France, and the female was never sent. Perhaps it had never even been captured and had been, somewhat optimistically, promised in advance. The male zebra arrived in France at Lorient in July 1786. The zebra was tethered to a coach and conveyed to Versailles, boarded at inns along the route. Three weeks later, the zebra arrived at Versailles. It was never joined by another.[25]

The aforementioned 'wild horse with zebra like stripes', however, could still be found at Versailles. This animal was, as it turns

out, a quagga – an animal that has, as noted, shifted in categorization from being a separate species to a subspecies of the zebra. It attracted very little interest at the time; after all, two zebras had been requested, not a drab wild horse. The quagga was nonetheless tenacious, becoming one of the few royal menagerie animals to survive the French Revolution, and be housed at the Jardin des Plantes in 1794. The skin of this animal can be seen today at the Muséum national d'Histoire naturelle.[26]

'The Queen's Female Zebra', engraving from the *London Magazine*, 1762.

The story of the 'Queen's Ass', or the zebra that belonged to Queen Charlotte, casts a different light on the zebra in the eighteenth century. In contrast to Percheron's zebra, we know very little about how Charlotte's zebras came to arrive in Britain. Queen Charlotte's zebras – almost certainly Cape mountain zebras – nevertheless moved through Georgian culture in an idiosyncratic way, leaving numerous traces. As well as fuelling the

ASSES OF THE GREAT BRITAIN.

John Jones, 'The Asses of Great Britain', 1764, satirical print.

work of several humorists, the two zebras became public representations of the queen and her son, George. In this capacity, the zebras became animals through which various public grievances and critiques could be voiced. One of the zebras also served as source material for one of the most famous artistic representations ever made of the animal: George Stubbs's painting of 1763.

In September 1761 King George III married the seventeen-year-old duchess Sophia Charlotte of Mecklenburg-Strelitz. The following summer, a belated wedding present – or half of it, at any rate – arrived aboard the HMS *Terpischore*. Sir Thomas Adams, the captain of the ship, had wanted to give a pair of zebras to the queen, but only the female arrived alive.[27] This zebra – the first of two owned by the queen – was housed in a paddock near

Buckingham House and exhibited to the public. For those who could not get close enough to see the zebra, a painting (now lost and not to be confused with Stubbs's painting) was made and hung in a stable nearby.

Though no charge was intended, the crowds that were attracted to the mews stable to see the zebra had a fee extracted from the Queen's Guard, who expected them to cough up a threepenny admittance charge. Angry letters were written to London newspapers, wondering how such a 'petit practice' could take place under the 'very eye of Majesty?' The Queen's Guard were eventually ordered to desist the taking of monies, with some guards even being dismissed (evidently to no avail – six years later, in 1768, visitors were still being squeezed for admittance).[28]

Soon after the queen's zebra arrived in London, the city's wits and satirists churned out a slew of ass-related songs, ballads and satires. One song was called 'The Asses of Great Britain', authored by 'FART-inando, the ASS-trologer. Such rump-related humour traded in cheap shots at the young queen. The highlight of one ten-verse song, for instance, was the lines, 'What prospect so charming? / What can surpass? / The delicate sight of her M—'s A–?' The enthusiasm with which the English press and public took to 'The Queen's Ass' did not escape the attention of foreigners, in this case the French philosopher Voltaire (1694–1778). In a letter to Jean-Jacques Rousseau written in 1766, Voltaire told him that he would be gossiped about 'as they do the Queen's zebra, the English love to amuse themselves with oddities of every kind but this pleasure never amounts to esteem'. Voltaire was writing around four years after the queen's first zebra arrived, though jokes about the zebra would endure for decades.

Queen Charlotte's son, the Prince of Wales, was a well-known spendthrift and attracted a great deal of censure in London's print and caricature culture. One caricature from 1787, for instance,

Broadsheet
advertisement
for the zebra
formerly
belonging
to Queen
Charlotte.

depicted the prince in a striped suit with the witty title, 'The Queen's A—'. Sartorial humour clearly captured the spirit of the day, for in the very same year the poet William Wallbeck penned a short poem, 'The Zebra and the Horse', on the same matter. The prince in his 'fine coat' was said to resemble the 'zebra, insolent and proud, kept in the King's menagerie'.

The reference to insolence relates, presumably, to the fact that Queen Charlotte's zebra was known for her temper and tendency to kick spectators. For this reason, perhaps, the first zebra was eventually given or sold to Christopher Pinchbeck, a clockmaker and friend of King George III, and subsequently toured in a menagerie. When exhibited in Oxford, it attracted curious observers, both town and gown, with *Jackson's Oxford Journal* informing its readers that

> of all the natural curiosities exhibited at this university, nothing ever drew the attention of the curious so much as the beautiful zebra lately belonging to Her Majesty and generally called 'The Queen's Ass'.

When this zebra died, it was stuffed and put on display at the Blue Boar Inn in York – quite a comedown from her salubrious accommodation at Buckingham Gate. This unfortunate series of events did not escape the notice of the Rev. William Mason who, in a snide letter to Horace Walpole in 1773, some ten years after the zebra first arrived in England, pondered the ignoble fate of the Queen's zebra. Mason had seen an advertisement announcing the arrival of the stuffed zebra at York:

> Pray do you not think the fate of this animal truly pitiable? Who, after having, as the advertisement says, 'belonged to her Majesty full ten years', should not only be exposed to

For this Day only.

To all who are possessed of a laudable Curiosity, and are desirous of in-
specting the striking Parts of the Creation.

There is to be seen, at the

The   BEAUTIFUL

Z E B R A,

O R

W I L D   A S S;

The Only One of the Kind ever seen in Europe.

It was brought from the *Cape of Good Hope*, in the Year 1762, by Sir THOMAS
ADAMS, and presented to Her Majesty (who has been graciously pleased to make a
Present of it to one of Her Domesticks) and has been shewn to most of the Nobility
and Gentry, adjoining the Queen's Palace ever since, with universal Approbation.

THERE is a noble Curiosity strongly impressed on the human Mind, which gains
Strength and Refinement by the Advantages of a liberal Education. Excited by
this excellent Principle the Wonders of the Creation are explor'd ; and the Learned,
struck with Amazement at their great Variety and Beauty, acknowledge the Works of
the Creator to be both manifold and marvellous !
This ZEBRA is an extremely beautiful Animal, and greatly surpasses all others for
Elegance, Symmetry and the Beauty of its Colouring. It is about the Size of a Mule,
but of a much more elegant Figure. The Head is small, the Ears are long, and the
Eyes are large and bright, The Neck is elegantly turned. The Legs are small and delicate, and the Tail long and beautiful. The whole Animal is party-coloured, or beautifully striped in a transverse Direction, with long and broad Streaks, alternately of a
deep, glossy, and shining Brown, White and Black. There is a fine Display of Elegance and Symmetry in its whole Form, and it is remarkable for Swiftness. The Beauty
of its Skin exceeds Description, and no other Creature can stand in Competition with it,
for it strikes every Beholder with a pleasing Astonishment. The Sacred Writings have
mentioned these Animals, particularly in *Job xxxix.* 5, 6, 7, and 8, and *Psalm civ.*
It is remarked, by the Curious, that this Creature (singular and beautiful as it is) was
brought from a Country whose Inhabitants are noted for Deformity and Ignorance :
And, it is the general Opinion of the Learned and Travellers, that no Country in the
known World has produced its Equal.

*** It is to be seen, by one or more, from Eight in the Morning, 'till Seven in the
Evening.

the close inspection of every stable boy in the kingdom, but her immoralities whilst alive thus severely stigmatized in every country newspaper. I should think this anecdote might furnish the author of Heroic Epistles [an allusion to Ovid's *Epistles*] with a series of moral reflections which might end with the following pathetic couplet; 'Ah beauteous beast! Thy cruel fate evinces. How vain the ass that puts its trust in Princes!'[29]

The advertisement to which Mason refers had said that the zebra was so vicious in life that 'she is better to be seen now than when alive'. When Mason used the word 'immoralities' to refer to the zebra's behaviour and character, he no doubt also intended a sexual undertone that referred back to jokes about the Queen's Ass – the ass that was now exposed to the 'close inspection of every stable boy in the kingdom'.[30]

The supposedly violent character of the zebra, and the salacious subculture that formed around it, are easily forgotten when faced with George Stubbs's portrait of 1763. How Stubbs came to paint Queen Charlotte's zebra is unknown – the painting was found in the artist's studio after his death, suggesting that it wasn't a commission – though it was hardly out of keeping with the artist's interests. Stubbs's fame rested on his exceptional representations of horses, and he clearly had a thirst for natural history and its painstaking portrayal in paint. Counting among his friends the anatomists William and John Hunter, Stubbs – no stranger to animal dissection himself – sought a hitherto unseen anatomical accuracy in his animal portraits, aligned to a strong sense of an animal's individuality. Though centred in the canvas, and seen from the side – as natural history illustrations usually are – Stubbs's zebra not only feels like the portrait of a specific animal, but one whose emotions we might be able to access.

Stephen F. Eisenman has written of how Stubbs's animals 'bear marks of weariness, anxiety and loss'.[31] His mountain zebra certainly strikes a melancholy pose, with a slightly deflated mane, flattened ears (usually a sign of distress in a zebra) and dark, glassy eyes. The real power of the image, however, lies in the contrast between the zebra and the verdant green landscape in which she stands, which deliberately eschews the enclosed paddock in which the zebra was kept. Was this Stubbs's attempt to re-create an African forest or a vision of the future, in which a domesticated zebra is imagined strolling through an English wood? Here is the zebra, in all its beauty, removed from the herd, from its mate and from its natural habitat, and deposited in a

George Stubbs,
Zebra, 1763,
oil on canvas.

foreign landscape, where it sticks out like a sore thumb. As if to exaggerate its loneliness, Stubbs allows plenty of space around the zebra, making the image as much about the absence of other zebras as it is about the presence of this particular one. Encountering the painting on a television show broadcast during the 1990s, the actor Alec Guinness summed it up thus:

> The most moving painting shown last night was, for my taste, Stubbs's 'Zebra in an English Glade'. The animal, brilliant in his [sic] black and white stripes, standing in beautiful profile, looked stiffly perplexed and lost among all the dappled greenery. A stranger in a strange land.[32]

Jacques-Laurent Agasse, *Zebra*, 1803, oil on canvas.

A fashion plate of a woman in a striped hat and dress, from *Journal des Luxus und der Moden* by Friedrich Justin Bertuch, 1788.

white within

If Queen Charlotte hoped that her second zebra might be better behaved than the first, she was to be disappointed. It became known for its 'ungovernable behaviour' and was, in time, removed from Buckingham Gate to the menagerie at the Tower of London.[33] Here the zebra grabbed a keeper with her teeth and threw him to the ground; he might have been trampled to death if he hadn't been able to make a hasty retreat. However, the zebra's temperament wasn't the sole reason she was removed from the queen's presence. Queen Charlotte's biographer, John Watkins, attributed the removal to the 'rudeness of the populace'. He might have been referring not only to the unbecoming conduct of the crowds that came to see the zebra, but to the stubborn and unseemly jokes about the 'Queen's Ass' that cannot have failed to reach the queen's ears.

Not all of the zebras in captivity in Georgian London were as ill-tempered as the queen's. A male zebra exhibited at the Exeter

'Change, a menagerie on the Strand, was said to have 'entirely lost his native wildness', becoming 'so gentle as to suffer children to sit quietly on his back, without any symptom of displeasure'.[34] Some eighteenth-century naturalists like Buffon and Sparrman, as we shall see, were of the opinion that, in the right circumstances, the zebra might be tamed. The English writer William Nicholson was more circumspect, expressing 'little hope' that the 'vicious' zebra could ever be of 'great service to mankind'. Yet, even Nicholson allowed himself some self-indulgent dreaming. If, per chance, the zebra *could* be used in the same way as the horse 'an elegance and variety would be added to the luxuries of the great and opulent'.[35]

By the late eighteenth century, knowledge about the zebra was diffuse across Europe: zebras moved through print in a profusion of natural history works and were admired as living animals in numerous royal, national or commercial menageries. In the next century, as European colonization of Africa intensified, attitudes towards the zebra that emerged in the eighteenth century would have more far-reaching, and calamitous, consequences.

3 Colonizing the Zebra

The nineteenth century proved a critical period in the history of the zebra. Catalogued, consumed, skinned, selectively bred, harnessed and hunted, nineteenth-century zebras reached new heights of visibility, and came under increasing threat. As large swathes of their natural habitat were caught up in colonial conflicts, dramatic and tragic results ensued, the most significant of which was the extinction of the quagga (also known as the quacha, quakkah, quahkah or couagga). At the turn of the nineteenth century, large herds of quaggas could be seen in southern Africa; as early as 1878 quaggas were no longer found in the wild.[1] Five years later – on 12 August 1883 – the last known specimen died in the Artis Royal Zoo in Amsterdam. Although Africans had long hunted the quagga for food, without European settlers, visitors and the creation of safari culture, numbers would never have decreased at the rate they did.

Europeans first reached the Cape of Good Hope in the late fifteenth century, but it wasn't until 1652, with the arrival of Jan van Riebeeck and the Dutch East India Company, that organized settlement began. The advantages of establishing a colony at the Cape were clear, since it was the major stopping-off point for ships travelling from Europe to Asia. Tired and hungry sailors became increasingly familiar with Cape Town, landing there regularly for fresh supplies and recuperation on

the way to or from India. Such visits might include short trips into the interior, but there was, at this stage, little confidence in the wider commercial potential of southern Africa, let alone great curiosity regarding the indigenous population, or flora and fauna. Just as the usefulness of the zebra would later be questioned, the usefulness of the entire region was continually contested. Having control of the Cape would always be seen as politically expedient, but until the discovery of gold and

Samuel Howitt, *A Zebra*, c. 1807, watercolour and pen.

from life   _cHs_

Hippotigris Quacha.
The quagga.

Charles Hamilton Smith, _Hippotigris Quacha_ (the quagga), c. 1837, watercolour.

diamonds in the late nineteenth century, there was always some doubt as to the benefits of colonizing southern Africa. When the British took over the region from the Dutch in 1795 (losing it in 1803, only to reclaim it in 1806), it was with the primary goal of keeping it out of the hands of the French, and not from any serious hope of making money out of the venture.

As several commentators have noted, Europeans made few attempts to get to grips with the southern African interior before 1750.[2] Travelling in the region was very difficult, not just because of encountering indigenous populations (chiefly the Khoikhoi, San and, in the east, the Xhosa), but the severe climate, lack of permanent sources of water and fear of disease. As a result, records rarely extend beyond the region of Cape Town. In the second half of the eighteenth century, however, explorers started heading inland, armed with scientific equipment, hoping to widen their knowledge of what was to them a largely unknown and unmapped part of the world. These included the Swedish botanist Carl Peter Thunberg (1743–1828), the Swedish naturalist Anders Sparrman (1848–1820), the Scottish botanist William Paterson (1755–1810), the French zoologist François Levaillant (1753–1824) and the Dutch polymath (soldier, naturalist, artist and linguist) Robert Jacob Gordon (1743–1795). Travelling into the interior in the 1770s and 1780s, these men left often copious records of their encounters, in which zebras invariably feature.

Anders Sparrman, a pupil of Linnaeus and assistant naturalist on Captain Cook's second voyage of 1772 to 1775, was the first to publish a full-length account of his travels, in 1783.[3] Sparrman did not travel especially far – at least compared with later explorers such as William Burchell – but his account, based on his journals, is one of the richest of its time. It was in July 1775 that he recalled his first sighting of

Charles Hamilton Smith, *Hippotigris Quacha* (the quagga), *c.* 1837, watercolour.

whole troops of wild *zebras*, called by the [Dutch] colonists *wilde paarden*, or wild horses. They were seen in large herds, and appeared very beautiful in their striped black and white livery. It is the skins of these that are generally sold at our furrier's shops by the absurd name of *sea-horse* hides.[4]

Like many eighteenth- and nineteenth-century travellers, Sparrman presumes that the quagga is a 'species totally different' from either the mountain or the plains zebra (both known then, simply, as zebras), and notes George Edwards's earlier error in mistaking the quagga for a female zebra. Seeing them in the field, he is able to establish that the animals keep 'in very different tracts of country, and those frequently very different from each other'. He also observes differences within so-called species, including 'trifling variations from each other with respect to their streaks, particularly down the legs'.

Sparrman's main concern with the zebra, however, would dominate the majority of nineteenth-century accounts of the animal: domestication. Here Sparrman, undeterred by the fact that indigenous Africans have clearly had no success, harbours no doubts. Both quaggas and zebras, he is sure, will one day be 'broken in for the saddle or harness' and will ultimately provide 'greater service' than European horses, owing to their fitness against diseases, familiarity with the terrain and climate, and apparent abundance.[5] 'They seem to be intended by nature for this country,' he states, holding special hope for the quagga, which is 'not to be equaled by any horse'. While noting that quaggas and zebras have small feet, and tend to be slower than horses, he is confident that 'frequent riding and exercise' will allow them to overcome these difficulties. Indeed, he claims to have seen a quagga 'driven through the streets in a team with five horses' in Cape Town, although he admits that experiments made

Anders Sparrman's mounted quagga foetus, Naturhistoriska riksmuseet, Sweden.

by a 'wealthy burgher' – in which a team of zebras responded to the harness with 'prodigious fury' – serve as a reminder that the process of domestication may take a little time.[6] He expresses particular bemusement that colonists haven't already made more progress in this sphere, a theme later taken up with gusto by British colonists, who took the fact that zebras weren't domesticated as proof that the Dutch were lazy colonists. 'The success of an attempt to domesticate animals that are naturally fierce or timid,' remarked the pompous statesman John Barrow in 1806, 'would seem to require more perseverance and patience, more labor, and more address, than fall to the share of a Dutch peasant.'[7]

Like most explorers, Sparrman couldn't leave the continent without taking a souvenir or two in the name of science. Among his many treasures could be counted 'a full grown foetus of a quagga, which I brought with me from the Cape, and keep stuffed with straw in the cabinet of natural history belonging to the Royal

Robert Jacob Gordon, *Burchell's Zebra,* 1777, watercolour with artist's notes.

Academy of Sciences.'[8] The specimen, a rare extant example of eighteenth-century taxidermy, can be seen today in the Naturhistoriska riksmuseet in Sweden, where it is considered one of the museum's treasures. In little more than a hundred years, such specimens – sad simulacra for the real thing – would represent all that was left of the quagga, a fact that would no doubt have surprised Sparrman and his fellow travellers, who had such great hopes for the animal.

It is in the travel account of the botanist William Paterson, published in 1790, that we find early indications of the zebra's subsequent sorry history. Paterson refers to 'several Zebras, which inhabit the mountain; but as they are not found in considerable numbers, shooting them is prohibited', a reference to the already dwindling numbers of mountain zebras in and around the Cape.[9]

Paterson was joined on this trip by Robert Jacob Gordon, who would write later of a visit to a mountain that 'takes its name from the large numbers of wild horses and zebra which formerly frequented it, but now there may be four or five, since they have trekked away or been killed.'[10] In the interior, however, Paterson had no qualms about shooting zebras, and tasting their meat which, unlike many Europeans (the Dutch settlers in particular, who thought it unclean), he deemed to be 'very good food'.[11] Jacob Gordon concurred, considering it 'very pleasant'.[12]

It is to Gordon – one of the more fascinating personalities of the late eighteenth-century colony – that we owe the most memorable visual representations of zebras made in this era. Gordon also had something of a way with words, as shown in his account of a zebra hunt in 1779, in which he describes the sound of a distressed zebra as being 'a howl like when a stone is thrown over freshly frozen ice'.[13] Gordon, a Dutch-born soldier of Scottish

Robert Jacob Gordon, *Cape Mountain Zebra*, c. 1770, watercolour, with artist's notes.

descent whose confused allegiances led him to commit suicide when the British took Cape Town in 1795, undertook six journeys into the interior between 1777 and 1786. The drawings, paintings and maps he made form part of the Gordon Atlas, now in the collection of the Rijksmuseum in Amsterdam.

The four paintings Gordon made of zebras and quaggas in southern Africa are probably the first detailed studies created by a Western artist showing zebras in their natural habitat. Two of the images also contain Gordon's notes, which reveal that he analysed the animals closely, making measurements and noting behavioural trends.[14] Gordon's paintings are nevertheless highly staged: his zebras are represented singly (though a herd animal, zebras are usually pictured alone), and were probably drawn from dead animals, with only a passing interest in anatomical accuracy.[15] The landscape in which his mountain zebra appears

Robert Jacob Gordon, *Burchell's Zebra*, 1790, watercolour.

is most likely a composite creation, with two groups of mountains framing the animal. This is nature tamed and simplified. Even the zebra's unruly spirit has been tempered: Gordon's zebras appear to be smiling, perhaps in anticipation of their presumed destiny as man's ally.[16]

Robert Jacob Gordon, *The Quakkah*, c. 1770, watercolour with artist's notes.

Increased knowledge about the wildlife of southern Africa invariably went hand in hand with destruction of their habitat. The arrival of the British in 1795 ushered in a new period of colonialism, raising the number of human settlers and ensuring almost constant conflict between competing factions. Captain Robert Percival (1765–1826) was among the men who helped take the Cape from the Dutch in 1795 and he stayed there for two years afterwards. His book *An Account of the Cape of Good Hope* was published in 1804, soon after the short-lived return of the Cape to the Dutch. Like many accounts published around this time, Percival's text is heavily biased against the Dutch settlers, and is convinced that the future of the region lies with the British, who he considers well placed to make best use of its natural resources. 'Should ever the Cape fall permanently into the hands of Great Britain,' Percival writes, 'those people [that is, the indigenous tribes] under proper management, may speedily arrive at a great degree of civilization.'[17] The same clearly applies to the zebra. 'That beautiful animal, of the horse species, called zebra, I have also seen quietly grazing in the fields above [Cape] town,' notes Percival:

> it is asserted by naturalists, that the zebra could never be tamed or brought to a docile and tractable state; yet I have myself witnessed the contrary; and can contradict the accounts of this animal's untameable disposition, from having seen him, with my own eye, as gentle and inoffensive as the patient ass, picking up thistles by the side of the road.[18]

Percival seems to be inviting his readers to re-imagine Cape Town as an extension of England, with the zebra replacing the donkey in a bucolic, managed landscape.

In the same year that Percival's book was published, the British artist Samuel Daniell (1775–1811) published the first of two volumes of aquatints called *African Scenery and Animals*, by far the most lavishly produced book yet detailing the wildlife and local customs of southern Africa. Daniell travelled extensively within the Cape of Good Hope between late 1799 and early 1803, joining an expedition led by the physician Dr William Somerville. His official position was that of secretary, though he was also a talented artist, from a family of respected traveller-artists (his brother William and uncle Thomas spent several years in India).[19] Daniell was said to have been a great admirer of George Stubbs, and it is clear from his book, and from related drawings, that he took the art of representing animals very seriously. Daniell's animals are located within a particular habitat and, although he drew from carcasses, he clearly observed animal behaviour in the wild, which helped him imbue his subjects with a strong sense of movement. Though he adopted the usual trend of situating a single animal, seen from the side, somewhere near the centre of the picture, he frequently introduced other animals or human figures in the background, freeing his images from the dry traditions of the natural history plate.

Zebras appear twice in Daniell's portfolio. The first appearance is in the final plate of the first volume. Titled *The Quakkah*, the image represents an adult quagga situated in a dramatic landscape.[20] Further quaggas are visible in the background, alongside eland and ostriches. The central quagga, whose bold curves are echoed in the mountains behind, strikes a curiously heroic pose, quite different from the scrawny quagga pictured by the artist and naturalist James Sowerby in the 1820s. Surely quaggas were never as roundly muscled as this?

Daniell may have been exaggerating for artistic effect; nevertheless, reports do suggest that the herds of quaggas encountered by travellers at this time were, in the words of Daniell's fellow traveller William Somerville, 'in high and plump order'.[21] Contemporary accounts often refer to very large herds of quaggas, and remark upon the animal's strength. Somerville writes of the 'sleek and smooth' skin of the animal, claiming that 'nothing can exceed the beauty of the coat the ground of which is a dark glossy brown, with yellow stripes'.[22]

The Quacha from his shape and muscular strength is remarkably well suited for hard labour, and from the great care with which he is fed and kept in condition might certainly be turned to important use in the purpose of agriculture, if the inhabitants had enterprise enough to domesticate and breed him . . . The quacha approaches nearer the Horse in his form than the Zebra does, his head crest and Ears are much like those of a punch made pony, his chest is broad and the limbs much stronger.[23]

Samuel Daniell, *The Quakkah*, 1804, aquatint engraving. Daniell's stocky quagga portrait was widely imitated by those who hadn't seen the animal in the flesh.

These words suit Daniell's image perfectly. Printed on the cusp of the second British occupation of the Cape of Good Hope, his

'Quakkah' is as much a vision for the future as it is a reflection of southern Africa as it was. This quagga is ripe for enterprise: on the threshold of domesticity and/or destruction.

Several writers have noted how animals in natural history illustrations of this period are pictured as if through the barrel of a gun. Daniell's proud, upstanding quagga may be pointing towards his destiny as a beast of burden, or he may simply be enjoying his last moments before slumping to the ground (the state in which he probably was when Daniell made this study). Indeed, the death (or again, domestication) of the quagga appears to be prefigured in the background of the same image, where a struggle between a man and a quagga is taking place, overseen by

James Sowerby, *Quagga Zebra*, c. 1824. This watercolour of a rather scrawny young quagga was probably based on a skin, as Sowerby never travelled to southern Africa.

Samuel Daniell, dedication from *African Scenery and Animals* (1804).

a saddled animal on the right. Three quaggas escape towards the hills on the left.

If this image suggests that the fate of the quagga is not yet sealed, Daniell's second volume of plates opens with a picture in which the zebra's predicament is rendered explicit. It was traditional for artists to open such books with dedications, often elaborately integrated within one of the images. Daniell duly dedicates his second volume to his friend David Davies, in lettering inscribed into the pelt of a skinned zebra, held aloft by two vultures. It is an arresting way to start a book, one which brings into the foreground the violent tableaux that take place in the margins of other images. Here the noble plumpness of his quagga has given way to the splayed hollowed-out body of a zebra, carrying a message of friendship between two men. While Daniell's party certainly shot their fair share of zebras, even they might not have anticipated the hunting culture that would develop in southern Africa over the course of the next century. There is no doubt, however, that books such as Daniell's inspired the next generation of European visitors, for whom the Cape of Good Hope was as much a sportsman's playground as it was a field of scientific discovery.

In the meantime, there was still much scientific work to be carried out. Leading the way in this regard was the British botanist William Burchell, who arrived in Cape Town in 1810. Burchell's subsequent trip into the interior of the region, begun in June 1811, was to last around four years, covering much uncharted land. Burchell kept detailed notes, made hundreds of drawings and collected around 60,000 specimens of plants, seeds, insects, fish, animal skins and skeletons on his travels.[24] He had hoped, upon arriving in Cape Town, that he might be the first to discover the unicorn, which many believed to be hiding somewhere in southern Africa.[25] This didn't quite work out, although Burchell did record several new species, most prominently the white rhinoceros (*Ceratotherium simum*). Burchell's name was subsequently attached to various southern African plants, and also to a subspecies of zebra, Burchell's zebra (*Equus quagga burchellii*), which was once thought to have been a separate species but now widely categorized as a branch of the plains zebra family.

While in the Cape of Good Hope, Burchell encountered many zebras, and made a by now familiar attempt to tame a quagga foal. He also recorded native uses for zebra skin, making a sketch which was later engraved for the published account of his travels:

My notice was attracted by the beautiful skin of a zebra, that had been formed into a *tanning vat*, supported by four stakes on a frame to which its edges were bound by thongs in such a manner, that the middle, hanging down, formed a capacious basin.[26]

The story of how Burchell's name came to be attached to the zebra is a complex one. Although Burchell was responsible for differentiating between mountain and plains zebras, and varieties therein, he did not deign to name either of the animals after himself. This honour was instead bestowed on him in 1825 by John Gray, keeper of the Zoological Collections at the British Museum in London. The gesture was not, however, made in an especially respectful spirit; it is in fact thought that Gray's creation of *Asinus burchelli* was a private joke, alluding to Burchell's difficult relationship with the museum. Burchell was a conscientious man, and doubted that the museum was treating his numerous specimens with the care they deserved. Gray, for his part, thought Burchell was being a bit of an ass.[27] Thus Burchell's name found itself permanently associated with the zebra.

William Cornwallis Harris, *Quagga*, from *Portraits of the Game and Wild Animals of Southern Africa* (1840). Though Harris saw quaggas in the wild, his portrait nevertheless drew heavily on Samuel Daniell's earlier image.

Shortly after Burchell returned from the Cape, the British decided to expand their southern African settlements, sending over several thousand people in the summer of 1820 with the hope of consolidating the eastern frontier. This brought the Cape Colony, previously seen as a temporary political possession, firmly into the public consciousness, and set the seeds for long-running conflicts with both indigenous populations and the former Dutch colonists. Fired by Daniell's images, and by Burchell's extensive writings about southern African landscape and culture, the next generation of imperial travellers was eager to explore the interior of the continent. One of the more prominent personalities was William Cornwallis Harris (1807–1848), a trained engineer and army officer, often credited as being the father of the modern safari.[28] Invalided to the Cape in 1836, following service in India, Harris set out on a hunting expedition that was to change the shape of big-game hunting in Africa, spawning several popular publications. The first line of *The Wild Sports of Southern Africa* (1852) encapsulates his approach: 'From my boyhood upwards, I have been taxed by the facetious with *shooting-madness*, and truly a most delightful mania I have ever found it.'[29] Harris's account is everything people would come to expect from a hunting adventure story, full of tall tales told in breathless purple prose, and accompanied by lively images. Like many hunters, Harris had a passion for wildlife that manifested itself in the desire to kill as much of it as possible. He was as comfortable writing about the beauty of zebras as he was about methods of slaying them.

Harris's *Portraits of the Game and Wild Animals of Southern Africa*, containing lithographic plates after Harris's own drawings, and first published in 1840, is a sumptuous production, containing several images of zebras, both skinned and alive, alongside some memorable written portraits.[30] Harris's quagga clearly echoes Daniell's earlier image, although he places it within a quieter landscape, and within a slightly larger herd. His mountain zebra is a rather more daring image, placing the animal on an elevated outcrop, with a klipspringer for company. The inaccessibility of the mountain zebra ('whisking their brindled tails aloft, helter-skelter, away they thunder down craggy precipices, and over yawning ravines, where no less agile foot could dare to follow them') is underlined so as to bring into relief Harris's skill in tracking it down.[31]

The fact that the zebra population seems to be dwindling is not lost on Harris; he notes, for instance, that the quagga 'was formerly extremely common within the Colony, but vanishing before the strides of civilization, is now to be found in very limited numbers, and on the borders only'.[32] This reality does not worry him unduly: the rarer the animal, the more exciting the pursuit. He is determined to enjoy African wildlife while it lasts, revelling in his own destructive powers. Action is crucial to Harris as an artist. If one animal is pictured stationary, another must be on the move. Scenes of animals hunting each other are juxtaposed with humans hunting animals. Harris relates how members of his party would dress themselves in the skins of those they killed: 'decorated with white and black plumes from the ostrich, the scalp and mask of the Zebra, *with the ears on*, formed the favourite head dress of our followers'.[33] The flattened skin of a plains zebra is illustrated, and appears also as part of a grisly pile of skins, skulls, horns and eggs. This picture clearly anticipates the loaded trophy cabinets of the countless imperial hunters to follow in Harris's footsteps, including such names as Roualeyn George Gordon-Cumming (1820–1866), Frederick Courteney Selous (1851–1917) and William Charles Baldwin (1826–1903), who all left best-selling accounts of their exploits. The image also finds its present-day counterparts in the countless images of smug and smiling hunters posing in front of dead zebras (often positioned

as if they are merely resting) available to anyone who cares to google 'zebra hunt'. Popular writers such as Wilbur Smith, meanwhile, speak to a continuing fascination with the colonial adventure story, with its distinctly uneasy mixture of sex, racial stereotyping and gratuitous slaughter of animals.

William Cornwallis Harris, 'Mountain Zebra', from *Portraits of the Game and Wild Animals of Southern Africa* (1840).

Perhaps the most famous hunting incident to take place in southern Africa in the nineteenth century occurred during the royal visit of Prince Alfred, Queen Victoria's second son, in 1860. Tribesmen were asked to gather together several thousand animals, including hundreds of zebras, within a particular cordon of land, so that the prince and his party could shoot without fear

Safari trophies from *Portraits of the Game and Wild Animals of Southern Africa* (1840).

of failure. Touted as the 'greatest hunt in history', it is better understood as a crass symbolic act, underlining the power of the British monarchy over its colonies.

Hunting African animals continues to attract modern-day princes, although Prince Harry's exploits in the field (in 2004 he was pictured leaning on the carcass of a water buffalo) are countered by his regular public denunciations of illegal poaching. Contemporary hunters, such as twelve-year-old Aryanna Gourdin – who infamously posted an image of herself sitting beside a dead zebra on Facebook in 2016 – prefer to refer to themselves as conservationists, arguing that the revenue created by trophy hunting creates essential funds for animal protection.

Just as Gourdin's activities attract widespread criticism today, nineteenth-century writers also questioned the ethics of hunting big game, as proved by an article published in *Parley's Magazine* in 1837. *Parley's* was an American periodical aimed at children, with a strong moralistic underpinning. Accompanied by an evocative (but not especially realistic) woodcut, 'Hunting the Zebra' pulled no punches when it came to Harris's favourite pastime, mocking the idea that killing exotic animals was 'noble fun':

I dare say it seems to you like noble fun; but how seems it, think you, to the poor zebra? Has not this animal feeling, as well you? Is he happy – is it noble fun to him to have a troop of men and horses at his heels, and the teeth of

Watercolour of a zebra shot 32 km (20 miles) south of the Zambesi, by Thomas Baines, *c.* 1860.

a cruel mastiff deep fixed in his limbs; to be frightened almost to death besides being hurt; and to crown all, to be made a slave, and carried several miles from home, and kept all the rest of his days in a strange country, and exhibited to people in a strange manner . . . How deep and mysterious is the perversity of the human heart![34]

The text takes on both hunting culture and the capture of wild animals for exhibition, enjoining its readers to 'learn to love all living beings, and try to make them happy as you can'. Such words largely fell on deaf ears, as the 'strides of civilization' continued to encroach upon African soil.

Those who lacked Harris's spirit of adventure found increasing opportunities to enjoy the sight of a zebra at home during the nineteenth century. In the 1820s an exhibitionist called Sheriff

'Hunting the Zebra', woodcut from *Parley's Magazine*, 1837.

Parkins was said to have driven a pair of quaggas through the streets of London. The Zoological Society of London, which was founded in 1826, purchased the first of several quaggas in 1831. Zebras were a common feature of menageries, both static and travelling, and were beginning to appear on country estates, such as Owston Hall near Doncaster. In 1828 the painter Ramsey Reinagle was commissioned to paint the animals of Owston, choosing in his colourful canvas to place them in a fictive African landscape rather than that of North Yorkshire.[35] What better way to show off your wealth and international connections than to have a small herd of zebras grazing on your front lawn?

Jacques-Laurent Agasse, *Quagga*, c. 1821, oil painting.

Among the other zebra collectors of this era can be counted George Douglas, 16th Earl of Morton. Douglas was a keen amateur scientist and member of the Royal Society. Like many members of the aristocracy, horse breeding was a subject close to his heart, and he was intrigued by the potentialities of the zebra. On this basis, he bought a male quagga, with the idea of breeding and eventually domesticating the species. Frustrated in his attempts to secure a female, he tried to breed his quagga with an Arabian mare instead, producing a horse–zebra hybrid. What happened next surprised everyone. Douglas sold his Arabian mare to a friend, who bred it with a black Arabian horse. The offspring of the two horses, however, bore a 'striking resemblance to the quagga'.[36] Could this be taken as proof of telegony, the idea that offspring bear the traces not just of their parents, but of their mother's previous partners also? Such was the claim that Morton went on to make in his influential essay, 'A Communication of a Singular Fact in Natural History', published in 1821. The case of 'Lord Morton's mare' became famous, and was for many years thought to have represented a breakthrough in reproductive science. Subsequent discoveries proved that Douglas was mistaken – and that the quagga-like qualities of the foal in question were actually a rare and coincidental reappearance of the horse's ancestral traits. For some time, though, the quagga found itself, not for the last time, at the centre of a major scientific controversy.

Domestication remained the key issue hanging over the zebra throughout the nineteenth century. Douglas seems to have abandoned his efforts to domesticate the quagga, but other men pursued it, even as the evidence stacked up against them. The idea that the zebra might turn out to be just as, if not more, useful than the horse gradually lost currency, but the temptation to ride in a zebra-drawn carriage, or to put zebras to practical use

as part of the colonial war effort, proved irresistible. In 1858 an American horse-tamer named John Solomon Rarey (1827–1866) best known for calming violent horses, turned his hand to the zebra, inspiring the following celebratory verses, printed in *The Ladies Cabinet of Fashion*:

Jacques-Laurent Agasse, *Male Quagga from Africa, the First Sire*, 1821, oil painting.

> What! He, the spurner of control,
> That never brooked the bridle yet?
> What! He, the fierce wild ass's foal,
> Whereon man never dared to sit?

He come and go at man's command,
Obedient as a poodle trained;
Rise at the raising of a hand,
By gentlest word or look restrained?

The human soul to him hath spoken,
But not in menaces and threats:
No stripes his stubborn will have broken,
No bondage his free spirit frets.[37]

According to the *Illustrated Times*, Rarey's zebra was presented
'before her Majesty, at the riding-school in the Royal Mews, a
subdued animal'.[38]

In 1860 the Acclimatisation Society of Great Britain was founded, and became famous for hosting dinners in which exotic animals, from eland to kangaroos, were served up. However it wasn't all about the fancy food: the Society sought to introduce, acclimatize and domesticate as many foreign animals as they could, taking advantage of the spread of the British Empire to achieve their aims.[39] *Punch* made good fun of their objectives, printing in 1865 an illustration by George du Maurier with the caption 'Probable Results of the Acclimatisation Society'. It is a typical Victorian London street scene, but in place of the usual horses, ponies and dogs, we find ostriches, giraffes, rhinoceroses, kangaroos and, right in the middle of the picture, a harnessed zebra.[40] A slightly earlier illustration from *Punch* shows Mr Punch himself riding on the back of a zebra. The caption reads, 'A Probability. "Hold Your Zebra, Sir?"'[41]

Such sources suggest that for some people it was still only a matter of time before zebras would be ridden through London. Countering this attitude were increasing reports that quagga numbers were declining rapidly. Already the animal described in 1804 as 'in high and plump order' was moving towards extinction, victim of its own docility in the face of firearms. When Sir George Grey (1812–1898) presented a quagga to the Zoological Society of London in 1858, it was received very gratefully, in the full knowledge that the animal might someday become a rarity.[42] This quagga joined another, acquired earlier that decade, which went on to have the unenviable distinction of being the only quagga photographed alive. At least five photographs of this female quagga have survived, taken between 1863 and 1870. The quagga died in 1872, roughly ten years before the 'last' quagga in Amsterdam. These photographs present a startling contrast with Samuel Daniell's illustration, made only sixty years before. Standing in a concrete yard, surrounded by bars and bricks, the quagga

is no longer the symbol of potential, but of humanity's capacity for destruction.

Sir George Grey's interest extended beyond the quagga. Grey served as Governor of South Australia from 1841–45, Governor of New Zealand from 1845–53 and 1861–8, and Governor of the Cape Colony from 1854–61, making him one of the most experienced colonial officers of the age. In 1862 he bought the island of Kawau, off the northeast coast of New Zealand's North Island. Here he tried to re-create aspects of all the regions he had lived in, importing animals and plants from all over the world. While it lasted (which wasn't very long; he sold the island in 1888), Kawau was a kind of microcosm of the British Empire, where kangaroos and possums rubbed up against English deer, emus, peacocks and, of course, zebras.

The most famous zebra fanatic in the late nineteenth century was probably Walter Rothschild, a wealthy and eccentric zoologist who founded the museum at Tring, in Hertfordshire, now part of the Natural History Museum. Rothschild opened his museum in 1892. Exhibits included a mounted quagga, purchased in 1889, one of only 23 remaining quagga skins.[43] As well as owning almost the full 'set' of skins, which graze together in tightly packed glass cases to this day, Rothschild also owned several live zebras, which he attempted to domesticate. Rothschild's zebras came to Tring in 1894, whereupon he began the process of breaking them in. Photographs exist of Rothschild being driven by a zebra in a single trap and in a larger, four-in-hand carriage, pulled by three zebras and a pony. It was in the latter contraption that Rothschild drove down Piccadilly and into the forecourt of Buckingham Palace, a deed that has since taken on mythic status. According to Rothschild's biographer, 'Walter himself admitted

Lord Lionel Walter Rothschild and his zebra-drawn carriage at Tring, 1895.

it was rather risky – his heart was in his mouth when Princess Alexandra tried to pat the leading zebra.'[44] H. A. Bryden wrote in 1896 that Rothschild's zebras were 'well broken, and are often to be seen in harness at Tring Park . . . as well as in London'.[45] It is hard to gauge from these accounts, however, whether the zebras served as an adequate replacement for horses, or represented a regular stunt. What we do know is that Rothschild took advantage of those occasions in which he did ride his zebras, making sure that a photographer was on hand to record the incident.

In these images, the fantasy of a zebra-drawn carriage is given glorious life. Note, however, how the pony that leads the carriage

The Rothschild zebras leading a four-in-hand carriage outside the Royal Albert Hall, c. 1898. Note the pony leading on the front left.

is positioned directly behind a zebra, to give the impression that the carriage is being pulled by four zebras. Such images do not prove that zebras are especially good at pulling carriages, merely that they can be trained to pull a carriage long enough for a successful photograph to be taken.

By the end of the nineteenth century, images of zebras pulling carriages, or taking part in races, were relatively common. In 1904 a company calling itself the 'East African Zebra Range' described itself as the first private enterprise dedicated to breaking in zebras for the international market, and held great hopes for the future of the 'zebrule' – a zebra and mule hybrid – which it believed would 'result in the production of a valuable adjunct to the World's means of transport'.[46] Zebras were also a regular feature in circuses, such as Herr Wolff's circus that played at Crystal Palace in the late 1890s, or the famous circuses of the German Carl Hagenbeck (1844–1913), whose use of wild animals was legendary. The dream of full-scale acclimatization or domestication, however, remained out of reach, both in southern Africa and back in England. Despite the best efforts of trainers, and a steady trickle of articles promoting its 'possibilities', the zebra was not about to replace the horse.[47] European intervention had not, as some had hoped it would, given the zebra a new sense of purpose. Zebras could now be found all over the world, but in their native land numbers were declining. Scientific research ensured that more was known about zebras than ever before, but understanding of the facts could not ensure protection of the species, as imperial expansion, territorial wars and hunting for sport, skins and sustenance all took their toll.[48]

The view from the turn of the century was not a remotely rosy one. In 1890 the British journal *All the Year Round* published an article titled 'The Downfall of the Zebra', which opened with the line, 'There is only too much reason to fear that one of the most beautiful animals in the world is rapidly becoming extinct.'[49] In his article of 1907, 'About Zebras', published in *The Western Field*, Laurence Irwell adopted a similarly melancholy tone:

> there are incontestable signs that the reign of the zebra group of quadrupeds is approaching a close . . . One form, the quagga, has already vanished completely; another, the mountain zebra, is approaching extinction, and even the most prolific of the group, Burchell's zebra, is being rapidly exterminated.[50]

By this time, calls for conservation were growing, and the opening of parks such as the Kruger National Park (opened as the Sabi Game Reserve in 1898) testified to a genuine desire to protect endangered species. As Jane Carruthers has noted,

> By the First World War, writing about wildlife in southern Africa had developed from a genre of sport and adventure to a literature that was beginning to take wildlife seriously as objects of ecological study and that burgeoned into conservation biology and wildlife management.[51]

There were distinct signs of a change in spirit. The welfare of the zebra, however, still ranked low on the priorities of those with power. In the second half of the nineteenth century, the commercial possibilities of southern Africa had expanded exponentially with the discovery of gold and diamonds in the north. The desire to control these natural resources far outweighed the desire to preserve local wildlife.

The creation of national parks and hunting restrictions clearly came a little too late for the quagga, whose demise in the wild

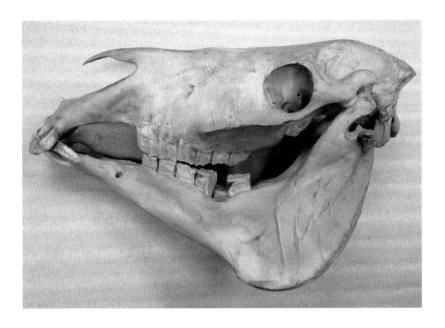

falls neatly between the discovery of diamonds in the late 1860s and gold in the 1880s, almost as if the fates had decided that at least one animal should pay the price for these breakthroughs. By the end of the century, the quagga existed in the form of skins and skeletons only, remains that would take on an almost mystical value (the natural historical equivalent of saintly relics). These specimens are now scattered across the world – although, tellingly, none of them can be found in southern Africa, where the animal originated. One such specimen is owned by the Grant Museum in London, and was recently subject to a major conservation project. Another specimen is owned by Yale University, having been purchased in 1873 by Othniel C. Marsh, the university's first Professor of Paleontology and a leading natural history collector. Subsequent tests would suggest that the Yale skeleton

Skull of the London quagga, now in New Haven, Connecticut.

was that of the quagga mare photographed at London Zoo earlier that decade. This same animal's skin would later turn up in Edinburgh, and can be seen today at the National Museum of Scotland.[52]

These specimens are not only relics of an extinct species, but – as recent events have shown – crucial resources in a project that seeks to address and mollify the dark legacy of the nineteenth century. Having been at the centre of a major scientific debate about telegony, the quagga is now, as we will explore in Chapter Five, at the centre of an equally compelling discussion over the possibility of restoring an extinct animal via selective breeding. Can the quagga be brought back from the dead? And if so, what are the implications of such an act?

4 Extraordinary Zebras

Anyone following the England cricket team in test matches over the last few years might have noticed the presence of zebras. Before a test series begins, it has become traditional for captains of the opposing teams to pose in front of a large plastic zebra. When play begins, it does so on a pitch emblazoned with a zebra or two. At some matches, spectators have been seen to be wearing zebra masks.

The omnipresence of an African equid around the England cricket team is a source of bemusement to many, though it is easily explained by the fact that the zebra is the primary logo of the banking company Investec, who in 2011 signed a ten-year deal to sponsor all home test matches.[1] Founded in Johannesburg in 1974, Investec has been listed on the London Stock Exchange since 2002. Hardly a well-known emblem of financial prudence, the zebra might seem a strange choice of logo. However, according to the company's client newsletter, the animal is a 'visual symbol' of the company's key philosophy, 'out of the ordinary', which highlights 'the unique nature of Investec and its clients', as well as pointing to its South African origins.[2] By drawing on the zebra, Investec clearly hopes to state its distinctiveness within the banking world, positioning itself as the exotic outsider among traditional British horses. Once again, the zebra's appeal lies in it being an extraordinary variation on an ordinary form.

'No dust, no grit, no hard work': Zebra Paste Grate Polish advertisement, c. 1890.

Though they are the most visible example operating today, Investec are not the first company to use the image of the zebra as part of a marketing strategy. In 1890 the company Reckitt & Sons – with roots in 1840s Hull – introduced to its long line of cleaning products something called 'Zebra Grate Polish'. The product itself was mundane – a black graphite-based paste used to brighten up a cast-iron fireplace – but the advertising campaigns built around it were colourful and lively. The use of the zebra, supposedly, related to the brilliant blackness of polished grates. None of this, however, was alluded to in the packaging and posters, which adopted a brave, essentially non-descriptive approach to marketing. One popular poster, for example, depicted a small zebra drawing two girls in a carriage along a dirt path in a deserted landscape. It appears to be raining, or has recently rained, a fact that doesn't seem to bother either the girls or the animal (who, for a harnessed zebra, is behaving very well). The only explicit reference to polish or fireplaces lies in the tins

The unlikely spectacle of young children driving a zebra-drawn carriage: Zebra Grate Polish advert, c. 1900.

Ceramic zebra candlesticks, designed in South Africa, by Ardmore Ceramics.

glimpsed in the basket of the girl on the right. Otherwise it is a surreal set-up, a curious mixture of homely Victorian sentimentalism and imperial adventure. Perhaps this is the point. The advert reinscribes Britain's international clout, bringing South Africa into the heart of the British home. A nation that can tame the zebra (even if, in fact, it can't) can certainly be trusted to produce a superior grate polish.

The British were not the only nation to appreciate the zebra's marketing potential at the turn of the century. In 1897 the Japanese businessman Tokumatsu Ishikawa founded Zebra Co. Ltd, a stationery company specializing in pens, which exists to this day (now with branches worldwide). Once again, the product has nothing to do with zebras, although the philosophy behind the company was apparently inspired by the animal's herd mentality. Ishikawa admired the zebra's solidarity in the face of danger, and the fact that the word zebra in Japanese can be written with Chinese characters composed of elements that symbolize 'writing' and 'royalty'. The company's trademark consists of a zebra looking backwards: 'to indicate that the knowledge accumulated in the past is being applied to make progress in new fields'.[3]

The attraction of the zebra to a modern advertiser is not hard to fathom. Zebras are distinct, eye-catching animals – on which basis the zebra image has been used to sell pretty much anything. As this chapter shows, zebras and zebra skin have, over the course of the twentieth century in particular, appeared in frequently unexpected places. As humans came to terms with the fact that the zebra could not be domesticated and de-exoticized – at least, not on any significant scale – they reasserted its status as an anomaly, an outlandish and increasingly rare animal that could be brought in to add a touch of mystery and/or sophistication to a product. In a century dominated by technological advancement, warfare and urbanization, the defiant wildness of the zebra attracted people who considered themselves outside of

Zebra-skin rugs, from Richard Lydekker's *The Horse and its Relatives* (1912).

the mainstream. Images of zebras, with varying relationships to the actual animal itself, began to pop up everywhere, from cricket pitches to cocktail lounges.

By the turn of the twentieth century, zebra hides had long been valued as a commodity. Although the zebra-skin trade does not seem to have peaked in the same way as ostrich feathers, there was always – and continues to be – a steady supply of hides leaving the African continent to be reconstructed as rugs and chairs. Contemporary examples of zebra patterning on furniture tend to be synthetic imitations; however, there are plenty of extant examples of real zebra-skin chairs. Most of these are heavy wooden affairs, consistent with the hunting lodge aesthetic – the kind of furniture that sits nicely under a trophy head, or next to a gun cabinet. Such furniture is still readily available on the Internet: for $1,000 you can have the hide of a zebra splayed across your floor as a rug, while a 'genuine Burchell Zebra hide wing-back chair' might cost as much as four times that.[4] An American supplier of zebra skins, Rojé Exotics, describes its zebra hides as 'absolutely stunning with a pattern of style and beauty that is unmatched in nature'. The company also caters for clients with qualms: 'for those of you who get turned off by looking at the head of the zebra we have a few without heads'.[5] The rugs, priced between $1,000 and $2,000, are made of zebra skins shot by trophy hunters who have paid thousands of dollars for the right to game hunt.

Zebra-skin furniture is not the preserve of hunting lodges. In the early twentieth century, modern designers also began to make heavy use of exotic animal skins. Here zebra hides served not so much as symbols of human mastery over the natural world, as chic accessories that suggested the barely contained wildness of their fashionable owners. The zebra provided an air of glamour in line with the stark black-and-white lines of art deco. Zebra print was elegant, sexy and looked very good in a clean modern interior. The Irish designer Eileen Gray (1878–1976), for instance, displayed zebra skin rugs in her apartment in the rue de Bonaparte in Paris, while an interior designed by the Russian-born British architect Serge Chermayeff (1900–1996) for the sculptor A. G. Grinling Gibbons in the 1930s juxtaposed the plain surfaces and straight lines of Modernist architecture with pseudo-primitive sculptures and a zebra-print chair.

Zebra print proved similarly popular among American designers in the first half of the twentieth century. The Californian-born Wayne McAllister (1907–2000) has been described as one of America's leading 'leisure architects', responsible for shaping the history of such national institutions as the drive-in restaurant, the casino and the cocktail lounge.[6] More Pop than Modernist, McAllister nonetheless shared Gray and Chermayeff's fondness for zebra print, making it the primary feature of one of his early designs, the 'Zebra Room' restaurant and bar at the Town House Hotel on Wilshire Boulevard in Los Angeles. The interior of this popular bar, which opened in 1937, and described itself in the 1940s as a 'favorite meeting place for Hollywood stars', included zebra-patterned chairs, table ornaments and tableware.[7] Murals covered the walls, showing zebras rushing across the savanna in the company of giraffes and monkeys. The scene would seem to be an imagined Africa, although it might have alluded to the presence of zebras in California, grazing in the private zoo of the newspaper magnate William Randolph Hearst (1863–1951), outside San Simeon. Descendants of Hearst's zebras can still be found in California today, nibbling the grasses around Highway 1.[8]

A slightly less fancy Zebra Room could also be found in Fort Shafter, the headquarters of the United States Army Pacific in Honolulu, Hawaii. This appears to have been a recreational space used by army recruits, featuring zebra-patterned chairs and, again, murals of African wildlife. The triangular stripes of the chairs at Fort Shafter echo, perhaps consciously, the striped insignia on the upper-arms of the non-commissioned officers. Other reports, however, link the name to a local jazz club or cocktail lounge, where musicians such as the pianist Dave Brubeck played in the 1950s.[9] The black-and-white stripes of the zebra clearly echoed – in this case as well as others – the keys of the piano, if not jazz music's reputation as music that brings together black and white cultures.

Other zebra lounges and bars can – and have been – found across America, from Clifton, New Jersey's 'El Zebra Club' to Washington, DC's 'Zebra Room' and Chicago's 'Zebra Lounge Piano Bar'. Clearly the character of the zebra is thought to be consistent with good food, good music and an 'exotic' night out. The presence of the zebra also serves as a mark of fashionable

The Zebra Room,
Los Angeles,
designed by
Wayne McAllister.

ZEBRA ROOM — THE TOWN HOUSE — LOS ANGELES, CALIFORNIA

ZEBRA ROOM
FT. SHAFTER

The Zebra Room at Fort Shafter.

eccentricity. Ju*Ju, an independent clothing store in Brighton, East Sussex, is painted with zebra stripes, the door guarded by a metal zebra head. This, along with the quasi-African name of the shop, prepares customers for the quirky 'vintage' items inside.

In all of these interiors, the presence of zebra print, and various zebra accoutrements, is unexpected, if not a little unsettling. The surprising combination of animal skin and modern furniture is probably best appreciated, however, in another product of the interwar period: Denham MacLaren's zebra skin armchair, now in the collection of the Victoria & Albert Museum (V&A) in London. Here authentic zebra skin is tightly wrapped around two cushions, squashed between two panes of industrial glass and screwed together by metal fittings. The near symmetry of the skin is exploited, although this order is disrupted from the back by the presence of two tufts of zebra mane (or possibly tail), offering an oblique reminder of the material's animal origin.

The so-called 'exotic, even Surrealist, touch' of the MacLaren chair is typical of the period in general.[10] Animal print – predominantly leopard, tiger and zebra – had been a fashionable feature as early as the eighteenth century. However, it was in the interwar period that it really took off, thanks in part to the success of the film *Tarzan the Apeman* (1932) and to the growing association between animal print and female independence. Leopard print, in particular, became closely linked with the public presentation of female sexuality, imbuing (mostly Western) women

Ju*Ju, a clothing store in Brighton, England.

with 'the excitement and adventure of the jungle' (see for instance the 'jungle girls' phenomenon, explored in our final chapter).[11] Initially the preserve of high-end fashion, animal print became gradually more common as the range of synthetic materials grew, and is now widely available on the high street, appearing almost exclusively on women's clothing.

Exceptions to this rule are usually comic ones, as in the tradition of the 'Masked Zebra Kid', a recurring figure in the world of professional wrestling based on a gimmick first adopted by George Bollas in the late 1940s (a title supposedly inspired by the striped stretch marks on Bollas's body). The comic-book character 'The Zebra' – whose name was inspired by the black-and-white

Denham McLaren,
Zebra Chair,
c. 1930.

prison uniform he assumes after being framed for a crime he didn't commit – appeared in several issues of *Green Hornet Comics* in the 1940s without ever taking off. Another comic-book from the same era suggests why this might have been the case. In issue eighteen of Fiction House's *Jungle Comics*, the zebra is described as the 'fashion plate of the plateaus': a 'snappy dresser' who 'flaunts his black stripes like any gigolo'.[12]

In this instance, the zebra (or zebra print) is considered incompatible with the narrow conceptions of modern-day masculinity. Such a conception is challenged, not only in the occasional advertisement (see Chapter Five), but in such works as Robert Giard's *Male Nude on Zebra Skin* (*c.* 1981). Giard (1939–2002) is best known for his photographic portraits of gay and lesbian writers, Long Island landscapes and nude figure studies. Writing of the latter, Giard noted his 'tendency to classicize and to abstract the human form' – evident in this almost-symmetrical portrait of an anonymous man, which draws obvious parallels between the skin and hair of the man and that of the animal on which he lies.[13] The zebra's mane almost runs into the man's hair, his beard into the black stripes of the zebra's back. Posing with an animal skin is usually an act of violent machismo; however, this is a disarmingly tender portrait – warmly as opposed to assertively provocative.

If leopard and tiger print hinted at the aggressive sexuality of the wearer, what did (and does) zebra print suggest? Are women in zebra print affiliating themselves with the legend of the untameable zebra, or is it just a matter of liking black-and-white stripes? A laughing Marilyn Monroe once posed in a zebra-print swimsuit with matching heels. The American singer Debbie Harry – celebrated for her punk, unconventional style – has been photographed several times in a zebra-print dress, most famously on the cover of *Zig Zag* magazine in 1978. In the 1990s, Madonna posed topless reclining on a zebra-print blanket. More recently,

Robert Giard, *Male Nude on Zebra Skin*, c. 1981.

the actors Cameron Diaz and Gwyneth Paltrow have shown a preference for zebra-print dresses, jackets, jump-suits and hand-bags, perhaps hinting that they are wilder than your average Hollywood actor.

While zebra print certainly shares the sexually suggestive overtones of leopard and tiger print, it has undoubtedly taken on meanings of its own. The most prominent of these, as noted above, is its association with Surrealism. The strange beauty of the zebra – the fact of its being horse- or donkey-like in shape, but differently marked – has made it especially appealing to artists looking to infuse their art with a sense of the uncanny. The zebra's refusal to fulfil the domestic role that humans have expected of it might have also attracted artists known for political and creative subversion. In this sense, the zebra becomes a metaphor for the artist, a figure that recognizes or epitomizes a certain type of beauty, while feeling that he or she doesn't quite belong.

The Argentine-born British artist Eileen Agar (1899–1991) was one of a few British artists to exhibit at the International Surrealist Exhibition in London in 1936. A painter, collagist, draughtswoman and sculptor, Agar was also interested in photography. A collection of more than eight hundred photographs left to the Tate reveals that among the many subjects that grabbed her attention during this period were zebras – both dead and alive. With an eye for the poetically bizarre, it is no wonder that Agar

Photographer unknown, *Eileen Agar Standing in Front of a Zebra Skin*, 1930s.

was attracted to zebras, and might even have identified with them. One photograph, taken in the 1930s, depicts the artist herself standing in front of a zebra-skin rug; in another, she poses with her friend, Mary Oliver, to whom the rug belonged. A third image shows Oliver wearing a tin hat, with a leg of the flattened zebra just visible to her right. The hat suggests that Oliver is assuming – and surely parodying – the role of the male imperial hunter. In all these photos, the zebra-skin rug is being used as an ironic prop, a token of offbeat humour that appears to speak to the artist's status as a social outsider.

Zebras reappear in the work of other artists associated with the Surrealist movement. For instance, the Italian artist Giorgio de Chirico (1888–1978) created several works featuring zebras from the late 1920s onwards. In each of these, the zebra is paired with a horse and placed on a beach within one of the artist's signature classical landscapes. The artist is perhaps alluding to the shared ancestry of the two species, drawing attention to the way in which animals with a similar form can have very different characters.

De Chirico might have been on Christopher Wood's mind when he set out to paint what many consider to be his final painting before his suicide in 1930. The Liverpool-born Wood (1901–1930) is remembered primarily for his landscapes and still-lifes, painted in a semi-abstracted style reminiscent of his close friend Ben Nicholson. Towards the end of his short-lived career, however, Wood was clearly channelling the work of such artists as the French painter Henri Rousseau (1844–1910). Wood's *Zebra and Parachute* (1930) depicts a zebra standing in front of a Modernist building, usually identified as Le Corbusier's Villa Savoye in Paris. The scene could easily be taken as an accurate representation of a European zoo (Berthold Lubetkin's Modernist penguin pool would open in London just four years later). The addition of

Christopher Wood, *Zebra and Parachute*, 1930, oil on canvas.

a drooping parachutist in the top right-hand corner of the canvas nonetheless provides the image with a Surreal twist.

Wood invites us to draw connections between the three elements of the painting: zebra, parachutist and architecture. Though it is likely that the work was not intended to hold any specific meaning, it is tempting to read the painting as an exploration of belonging. The zebra, like the parachutist, has been dropped into a landscape in which it doesn't belong. Or does it? The black-and-white lines of the zebra's coat, as we have already seen, were actually rather popular with Modernist designers and, it could be argued, fit as well here as they do within the lush greens and yellows of the African savannah. And yet this zebra, rather like the zebra in George Stubbs's painting of 1763 (to which Wood surely alludes), strikes a rather melancholy pose – although Wood's zebra's ears, unlike Stubbs's, are pricked. Like the parachutist above, it is alone: imprisoned by man, but also inaccessible – the eternally enigmatic zebra.

It is not known whether Wood identified with the zebra in his painting. It does seem, nevertheless, as though the zebra became something of a totem for several other British artists during this period. A zebra head appears many times, for instance, within the work of the young Lucian Freud (1922–2011), most prominently in two paintings, *The Painter's Room* (1944) and *Quince on a Blue Table* (1943–4). Freud owned a zebra head, given to him by his lover Lorna Wishart, and apparently purchased from Rowland Ward Ltd, a leading taxidermy company in London. Ward had a long history of producing zebra-based products, ranging from the standard mounted heads to zebra-hoof inkwells and decorative containers, examples of which are still available on the market. At least one edition of Rowland Ward's best-selling book *Records of Big Game* (first published in 1892) was adorned with a zebra-print cover. Freud, who had long admired – and drawn – portraits of horses and other animals, made good use of this unusual gift, positioning it in such a way that its truncation is obscured. In *The Painter's Room* (1944), the head forms part of a distinctly surreal tableau: painted with red stripes instead of black, the giant zebra pokes its head through a window into a room featuring a tattered sofa, a piece of red cloth, a black hat and a palm tree. In *Quince on a Blue Table* (1943–4), the zebra looms over a blue table, a couple of quinces and a torn paper bag. Photographs of the zebra head also exist: in one, the artist's daughter Annie, aged about two, sits beside the head; in another, Freud himself, wearing a suitably striped sweater, poses with the head on a sofa, stroking the nose as if it were alive. As with Agar's photographs, this image subverts the imperial hunter stereotype. Freud's attitude to the zebra trophy is not one of human triumph over nature, but of a tender relationship with a fellow creature (albeit one that died many years before). The great age of Victorian taxidermy was over, and objects like zebra heads were now just as likely to be found in the studios of young artists as they were on the walls of a country house. Shortly before his death in 2011, Freud was introduced to a live zebra in a short film, *Small Gestures in Bare Rooms*, by the director Tim Meara. Freud 'wasn't remotely interested in being filmed', Meara explained, but couldn't resist the 'exciting opportunity to meet a zebra'.[14]

Another British artist who frequently painted zebras was Mary Fedden (1915–2012). Best known for her brightly coloured still-lifes, Fedden enjoyed representing what she once described as 'quirky juxtapositions', merging the objects around her with those she saw on her travels.[15] One of the earliest appearances of a zebra in her work is the painting *Still-life with a Staffordshire Zebra* (1946), which depicts a ceramic zebra (large numbers of which were produced from the nineteenth century onwards) standing in front of a jug of flowers on a windowsill overlooking a London street. In later works, the Staffordshire zebra is replaced by what seems to be a real zebra, often accompanied by a human companion. Some of these images relate to 'distant memories' of a trip Fedden took to Africa, combined with her knowledge of Mansur's painting of Jahangir's zebra in the collection of the v&a (and perhaps Stubbs's painting also).[16] They all share a surreal quality, representing scenes that exist outside of everyday life.

The strange appearance of a zebra in a painting by Carel Weight (1908–1997) is more easily explained. On 27 September

Lucian Freud,
*Quince on a Blue
Table*, 1943–4,
oil on canvas.

1940, London Zoo was hit by several bombs, one of which landed on the Zebra House. No animals died, though two wild asses and a zebra escaped, the latter making it as far as the streets of nearby Camden, where it was chased by several zoo attendants and a keeper in a motor car. Kenneth Clark, then director of the National Gallery, thought it might be a good idea for an artist to record the episode.[17] He settled on Weight, who had a track record of painting works in which something surreal occurs in an urban or suburban setting. As Weight had not personally witnessed the zebra escape in September 1940, his commission was an imaginary scene, albeit based on real events. *Escape of the Zebra from the Zoo during an Air Raid* consists of four parts, rather like a painted comic book, charting the zebra's emergence from the fiery bomb wreckage and subsequent flight across London. In each of the paintings, the zebra, whose black-and-white coat stands out strongly against the red and brown landscape, enjoys its unexpected freedom.[18] As London burns, the zebra provides a flash of light, perhaps even a flash of hope, amid the chaos.

When the Australian-born artist Sidney Nolan (1917–1992) visited Kenya in 1962, he was struck by the extent to which the animals looked 'like new works of art – shining as if they'd just been painted by someone whose name I didn't know . . . the fascination of going to see a zebra or a gazelle is the fascination of discovering a perfected shape'.[19] Although Nolan would have witnessed zebras moving in herds, he followed artistic tradition in painting one alone, grazing in a markedly barren and dreamy landscape. His *Zebra, 1963* (private collection) – with stripes more brown than black – quite literally glows, despite its rather awkward pose and scruffy coat.

Nolan's image provides an interesting comparison with the work of his contemporary, the Hungarian-French artist Victor

Carel Weight, *Escape of the Zebra from the Zoo during an Air Raid*, c. 1940, oil on canvas.

Vasarely (1906–1997). Vasarely's attraction to zebras lay almost entirely in the patterning of their skin, which formed the basis for multiple works that are seen now to have been among the earliest examples of 'Op Art' (art that makes heavy use of optical illusions). Vasarely's zebras are heavily abstracted, reduced to uniform bands of black and white and joined together like pieces of a jigsaw puzzle, reminding us of the Comte de Buffon's comment regarding the zebra: 'one might almost imagine the rule and compass to have been employed in their distribution.'[20] In one of Vasarely's earliest zebra works, made in 1937, a stallion appears to be launching himself upon a mare. The violent subject, however, seems to be no more than an excuse for a play on the potential clash of black-and-white bands. Vasarely's jazzy, curvaceous – and much imitated – zebras dance through flat abstract landscapes, a long way away from the greens and yellows of their natural habitat.

Newspaper article on bombing of the Zebra House at London Zoo, 1940.

The Italian-born artist Ugo Mochi (1889–1977) also gravitated towards the zebra, finding in it the perfect subject for an artist working purely in black and white. From 1928 Mochi was based in the U.S., and in 1969 received his most important commission from the American Museum of Natural History in New York: a series of fourteen 2.5-m (8-ft) panels designed for the museum's restaurant. In the last few years of his life, he worked closely with writer and naturalist Dorcas MacClintock on two books, *A Natural History of Giraffes* (1973) and *A Natural History of Zebras* (1976). Mochi's intricate images, cut from one sheet of black paper with a lithographer's knife, capture zebras in a variety of ways, from standard, static natural-history side views to lively set pieces involving several animals. Mochi's zebras are rare in

Ugo Mochi, *Zebra,* from *A Natural History of Zebras* (1976).

being grounded in a close knowledge of the animal and its history, rather than a projection of personal fantasies of the exotic.

If one thing unites contemporary artistic representations of the zebra, it is the continuing influence of George Stubbs's painting of 1763. Works by diverse artists such as Ian North, Rodney Pople, Kathi Packer, Michael Joo and Rory Carnegie have all responded directly to Stubbs, with particular reference to themes of identity, celebrity and Surrealism.

In North's work of 1987, *Pseudo Panorama, Australia 1. (Zebra)*, a collage of two photographs, the zebra is adapted and transposed into an enlarged South Australian landscape, where it becomes almost camouflaged amid the undergrowth. The zebra is, as North notes, 'doubly displaced, being painted in London as if in an English forest or park surreally different from her South African homeland, then borrowed by me and again taken a long way from home, a virtual victim of the Enlightenment and an analogue for the processes of colonisation'.[21] *Stage Fright* (2008), a painting by another Australian artist, Rodney Pople, recasts the mountain zebra in Stubbs's work as a stage-struck celebrity, shrinking away from the limelight. In Pople's *Summer 1888* (2015), Stubbs's zebra reappears in a golden glade, bathed in warm sunlight, the title an ironic reference, perhaps, to the celebrations surrounding the centenary of the First Fleet arriving in Australia.

Connecticut-based artist Kathi Packer has also returned frequently to the zebra theme. In her painting *Stubbs's Curiosity*, from 2003, she transports Queen Charlotte's zebra once again, this time into a South American rainforest. Stubbs's painting, she realized, contained an unrepresented human presence; people were heavily implicated in this animal's life, despite it being pictured alone. She draws attention to this by including two figures (a double self-portrait) in her painting, dressed in black and white and seated on the zebra's back. The zebra's role as a fashion icon is highlighted – and the cost of its beauty indicated by the manner in which the black high heels of the models (whose melancholy gazes echo that of their ride) press sharply against its striped flank. In more recent work, Packer has responded to zebras in the wild, the experience of which was to her dramatically different from zebras in zoos or pictures. Zebras, she noticed, were constantly talking and twitching, swishing their tails and shaking their manes. These were not silent animals, but deeply social creatures, with lively temperaments. Rather than sticking out of the landscape, they were very much part of it.

The New York-based artist Michael Joo tackled Stubbs's painting in three related sculptures first exhibited in 2009. In *Stubbs (Absorbed)*, he created a life-size bronze zebra, striped black-and-gold rather than black-and-white, and positioned in front of a painted screen. The artificiality of Stubbs's landscape is highlighted – so, too, the kitsch value of the animal. As one reviewer noted, 'there is a palpable vulgarity to this art zebra, a sickness in its sheen. Nature can be ugly, but it's never vulgar. That's the domain of culture.'[22] In *Consistent-Seen-Touched*, the same zebra reappears, this time miniaturized and placed like a medical specimen on a stainless-steel tray, emphasizing both the solitariness of the original, and its fascination for scientists. In the final work, *Doppelganger (Pink Rocinante)*, Joo exhibited the mould used for casting *Stubbs (Absorbed)*, painted a lurid pink. The title refers back to another equid, perhaps hinting that the line between the pristine zebra and the hoary horse is thinner than we might believe (Rocinante being the name of Don Quixote's aged mount).

Finally, Stubbs's image also haunts the work of two contemporary photographers. Looking at Stubbs encouraged the British photographer Rory Carnegie to think about disconnections between animals and their habitat. In a recent series, titled *Long*

Ago and Far Away, he played with this idea by merging photographs of exotic animals living in the United Kingdom with photographs of their 'native' landscapes. Stella, a Chapman's zebra from Cotswold Wildlife Park, appears at first glance to stage a return to the African plains. However, it turns out that the landscape behind her is actually that of Burgess Field, a conservation area alongside Port Meadow in Oxford. The idea of placing a zebra in this landscape was inspired by the discovery of animal bones in the area, suggesting that exotic species such as hyenas, tigers and rhinoceroses may have once lived there. This served as a reminder that all native habitats are in a sense temporary, and controlled by the vicissitudes of climate. The question of where an animal truly belongs remains a complex one. The serenity of Stella in Carnegie's photograph reflects, again, the static side-on poses found in natural-history illustrations – a pose that presents particular challenges to the photographer. 'Zebras are very twitchy,' as Carnegie has noted, and don't respond well to studio lighting. It took up to five weeks to get Stella comfortable with the equipment, after which she granted the photographer about five minutes shooting time.[23]

The South African photographer Daniel Naudé has also gone to great lengths to photograph African animals, in a deliberate attempt to echo earlier representations by Stubbs and, especially, Samuel Daniell. In 2010 Naudé re-created Daniell's journey of 1801 from Cape Town to Dithakong, photographing animals he encountered along the way. Although the animals Naudé met were very different – mostly feral or domesticated – he sought to capture them in a similar way, drawing attention to the way that animals reflect the culture and identity of contemporary South Africa.[24] His *Quagga* differs greatly from Daniell's, which was proudly centred in front of a sweeping South African landscape: Eden on the verge of destruction. In Naudé's image, the destruction

has been and gone, and this one 'quagga' is all that is left: still centre stage, but standing under distinctly cloudy skies.

Rory Carnegie, *Stella in Burgess Field*, 2015, photograph.

As this chapter has shown, images containing zebras clearly operate in different ways, trading off various qualities we associate with the animal: singularity, beauty, defiance and melancholy. In some cases, the zebra is employed to give a touch of quirky exoticism; in others, to highlight wider political concerns. What remains clear is that, in the sphere of art at least, the zebra shows no sign of extinction, proving as attractive to artists and advertisers now as it ever was.

5 Stripes

In the early 1930s, Gladys Davidson, a Fellow of the Zoological Society, wrote *At Whipsnade Zoo* (1934). This children's guide to Whipsnade features a talkative zebra expounding the virtues of his 'smartly striped' coat. John and Jane, after being led to a 'first-rate picnic place' by a friendly wallaby for a 'jolly picnic' of cakes and sandwiches, approach Spicer's Field and spot a 'handsome zebra' by the railings. Jane, while proffering sugar lumps in her hand, is puzzled and tells the zebra that 'your striped coats are certainly beautiful, but I don't see how they could be useful when you hear the roar of a lion'. John, her brother, having been chosen as a budding naturalist by the author, helpfully ponders aloud, 'I suppose it is because they are so dazzling?' John has hit the nail on the head. 'Exactly,' replies the zebra. 'In the strong, clear-cut lights and shades of the African moonlit wilds a zebra is not easily noticed, because his vivid stripes mingle so wonderfully with his surroundings that he seems to be merely a part of them.'[1]

John's supposition – and, indeed, that of Gladys Davidson – is one that has been held by many through history. However, as this chapter will reveal, a reading of the zebra's stripes as dazzling camouflage is no longer as certain as this charming dialogue suggests. In fact, recent exhaustive field and laboratory research indicates that zoologists should look elsewhere to determine the function of zebra striping and its evolutionary drivers.

The idea that zebra stripes play an important role in crypsis, the ability of an animal to camouflage itself and avoid detection, had considerable force in the late nineteenth and early twentieth centuries. Alfred Wallace, an authority on natural selection and zoology, turned to the matter of the origin and uses of colour in animals in *Darwinism: An Exposition of the Theory of Natural Selection* (1889). Wallace considered the conspicuous markings of the zebra to be an example of glaring coloration for the purposes of recognition at long distances and concealment at a short distance:

> It may be thought that such extremely conspicuous markings as those of the zebra would be a great danger in a country abounding with lions, leopards, and other beasts of prey; but it is not so.[2]

Shortly after Wallace, the American naturalist and artist Abbot Thayer (the so-called 'father of camouflage') published his theory on countershading that became known as 'Thayer's law'. This law determined that many animals have evolved coloration to cancel out the shading created by the overhead sun. Thayer provided both the illustrations and the ideas that were published by his son, Gerald Thayer, in *Concealing-coloration in the Animal Kingdom* (1909). Here Gerald Thayer said of the zebra, 'among all the bolder obliterative patterns worn by mammals, that of the zebra probably bears the palm for potency and beauty'. Thayer used photographs of experiments that he had conducted to illustrate his theories on the obliterative coloration of the zebra. Cardboard model cut-outs of zebras were 'placed amid straws and imitation reeds or grasses, artificially arranged' to mimic the zebra in nature. Thayer considered the stripes to play an important role in 'wedding him [the zebra] to the strong and manifold striations of the vegetation all about him'. He concluded that the zebra's pattern 'cuts its wearer's aspect to pieces' and only failed to be obliterative when seen against a 'perfectly plain background'. It was this line of reasoning that would come to bear on the development of dazzle patterning in the First World War.[3]

John Graham Kerr held the chair in zoology at the University of Glasgow between 1902 and 1935, and had not only met Abott Thayer in person but had been forwarded a copy of the Thayers' book in 1914. On these grounds, among others, maritime historians Hugh Murphy and Martin Bellamy argue that it is Kerr, and not the marine artist Norman Wilkinson, who should be credited with introducing the concept of dazzle painting to British shipping during the First World War. Wilkinson proposed that a ship ought to be painted in such a way that its form was broken up – and in 1917/18 the Admiralty accepted his proposal. After the war, Wilkinson received official recognition as the inventor of dazzle camouflage, despite Kerr's counter-claim. We know that Kerr had received and read a copy of *Concealing-coloration in the Animal Kingdom* and would have seen the Thayers' photographs of their zebra experiments. Kerr wrote to Winston Churchill, First Lord of the Admiralty, on 24 September 1914, proposing that ships be painted with 'compensating shading' and that the continuity of a ship's surface be broken up. He followed this up with a natural historical analogy:

A giraffe or zebra or jaguar looks extraordinarily conspicuous in a museum, but in nature, when not moving, is wonderfully difficult to pick up, especially at twilight. The same principle should be made use of in painting ships.

Murphy and Bellamy have shown that the admiralty did, at least initially, respond positively to Kerr's proposals and implement dazzle patterning on an ad hoc basis; in 1915 HMS *Viking* was even referred to as a zebra after being 'painted in a coat of striped camouflage'.[4] However, Churchill moved on from the Admiralty and once his successor, Arthur Balfour, determined that warships be painted in a uniform grey, the few ships that had been dazzle-painted in line with Kerr's proposal were repainted. Later, in 1917, Norman Wilkinson proposed that ships be painted in blocks of strong colour to distort the vessel's form. Wilkinson's suggestion was enthusiastically adopted, suggesting a sea change in the Admiralty's attitude. In later years, Kerr would maintain that his proposed dazzle painting had been bungled and haphazardly applied (thus, naturally, the Admiralty had dismissed his otherwise sound idea).

A satirical cartoon, drawn by George Morrow and published in *Punch* on 7 April 1915, must surely have been inspired by contemporary experiments with dazzle patterning. A zebra at the zoo is half-painted in stars – a visual nod to the American stars and stripes – and accompanied by the caption, 'remarkable case of protective colouring. Owing, it is believed, to the fears of a German invasion, a zebra at the zoo assumes a neutral aspect.'[5] The target of *Punch*'s satire is far from camouflaged – even in the face of a German invasion of Britain, the United States was still neutral.

The success of dazzle painting remains difficult to determine, although Admiralty statistics suggest that dazzled ships struck by torpedoes were significantly less likely to sink than conventionally painted ships. This could suggest that enemy submarines found it difficult to determine the exact speed, course and form of dazzle-painted ships.

Later in the twentieth century, black-and-white stripes were once again selected by a British government ministry, but this time on account of their overtly conspicuous nature – and not any

obliterative or dazzling effects. Zebra crossings were not intended
to fade into the background of the urban environment, but
proudly proclaim their presence.

The 'zebra crossing' – referring to black-and-white longitu-
dinal stripes painted upon the surface of the road – was developed
in the late 1940s by the Ministry of Transport in an attempt to
reduce pedestrian fatalities. The first zebra crossings were trialled
in 1949 at test sites across the UK, and in 1951 stopping at a zebra
crossing was made a legal requirement for motorists. James Callaghan, Prime Minister of the United Kingdom from 1976–9, was
at this time Parliamentary Secretary to the Ministry of Transport
and – so the story goes – played an important role in the development of the zebra crossing. Callaghan was shown full-scale
models of a zebra crossing by civil servants in the ministry of
transport and persuaded Alfred Barnes, Minister of Transport,
to introduce the initiative.[6] Callaghan is even thought to have
coined the name 'zebra crossing', on remarking upon the resemblance to a zebra, but although he recalled expressing interest in

the crossing at the Transport and Road Research Laboratory, he could not confirm, when interviewed in the 1980s, whether he came up with the term or not.[7]

Perhaps the most famous zebra crossing in the world is the one painted on Abbey Road, northwest London, which featured prominently on the cover of the eleventh studio album of the Beatles, also called *Abbey Road* (1969). This iconic crossing (which, one supposes, must be regularly repainted owing to its unusual level of traffic) was given a Grade II heritage listing by English Heritage, now Historic England, in 2010. Grade II designates a structure of special interest for which efforts must be made to preserve it for posterity.[8]

Zebra crossings as a whole, though, are somewhat of an endangered species in the UK. Although zebra crossings had been seen on Britain's roads for some sixty years, between 2006 and 2011 more than 1,000 zebra crossings were replaced with higher-tech crossings – crossings with sensors and lights. The Automobile Association's Head of Road Safety, Andrew Howard, attributes this to motorists no longer stopping at zebra crossings in the

Zebra crossing.

Georges Barbier, 1912. A fashion plate of a woman in zebra-esque-striped dyed fur from *Journal des dames et des modes.*

G. BARBIER 1912

Manteau de Zibeline à col et poignets de renard blanc

absence of a red light, and pedestrians being wary of crossing without a signal. Plain zebras – plain zebra crossings, that is, not plains zebras – have thus disappeared from many city-centre roads. 'I'm struggling to think of a single plain zebra in Basingstoke,' reported Howard to *The Guardian* in 2011.[9] The future for the plain zebra crossing on British roads appears to be bleak.

Zebras can still be regularly spotted on the high street, however: as noted in the last chapter, there is a long history of zebra print in twentieth-century fashion. The cover of *Vogue* in January 1926 featured an illustration of a woman riding a red-bridled zebra, wearing an emerald-green dress and a long billowing veiled hat; in the background, three giraffes stroll across a palm-tree-dotted landscape. *Vogue* was on safari. This fashion illustration by André-Edouard Marty was, perhaps, inspired by a photo of the American-documentary maker, photographer and writer Osa Johnson taken in Kenya, at the base of Mount Kenya, in 1921. Johnson, wearing shorts, a hat and bobbed hair, is riding a tamed zebra on her first trip to Africa. Martin and Osa Johnson's first African expedition led to a film titled *Trailing Wild African Animals* (1923). Osa Johnson's autobiography, *I Married Adventure* (1940), was subsequently published with a zebra-striped cloth cover. The Johnsons bought an aircraft in 1932, a twin engine s-38Bs, and had it painted in zebra stripes. The plane was dubbed 'Osa's Ark'.[10] Johnson was already well known to Americans in the early '20s, so *Vogue*'s zebra cover was a nod to the exotic allure of the safari and the feminine appeal of the zebra. Zebra stripes, and even zebras, continued to appear regularly in fashion editorials in print throughout the twentieth century to the present day.

The sex appeal of the zebra is usually associated with women, with some notable exceptions. The American singer Adam Lambert, for example, was photographed in 2015 for an interview with *Schön!* magazine wearing a zebra-striped suit and other monochrome clothes, along with a taxidermy zebra head known as 'Mitsy' ('a very stubborn Zebra'). Lambert and 'Mitsy' appear to be in some kind of domestic bliss photographed together on a curved sofa, brushing their teeth in a bathroom and in bed (for clarification, 'Mitsy' is positioned tucked under the bedclothes, while Lambert sprawls out on top).[11] The photographs, by Diego Indraccolo, have a touch of melancholy to them as 'Mitsy' is the 'stubborn' prop in an ersatz relationship. Her dark, glistening glass eyes stare out at the camera. The zebra became a target of envy and wishful aspiration for fans on social media, 'Ich will das Zebra sein' (I want to be the zebra), 'zebra goals' and 'Soo jealous of that zebra!!!' being representative of responses to the photoshoot.[12]

Zebra print straddles cheap kitsch and high fashion, and can be found on any part of clothing, from hats to socks. In Aussiebum's 'Savannah' range, a herd of zebras can be seen galloping across a pair of men's swimming trunks, while Victoria's Secret offer a range of zebra-related underwear for women. You can find zebra print on Christian Louboutin's or Jimmy Choo's pumps and kitten heels, or on silk Hermès scarves (printed with the image of a winged zebra). In 2011, the windows of Louis Vuitton's Bond Street store were filled with life-sized zebras clasping luxury handbags in their hooves, balancing luggage on their backs or carrying couture-wearing mannequins.

The British designer Paul Smith is especially well known for his colourful striped designs and love of zebras. Their appeal, he says, is that 'they look like horses wearing pyjamas.'[13] Some of Smith's printed T-shirts feature zebras with multicoloured stripes; these sartorially idiosyncratic zebras draw envying looks from their boring monochrome brethren ('Is that a Paul Smith coat?', asks a zebra, green with envy). A Paul Smith children's jumper has an embroidered multicoloured zebra walking across

a zebra crossing, and a baby's bib features the much-loved 'Z is for Zebra'.[14]

Fashion editor Rebecca Willis recently reflected on the popularity of animal print after a restaurant dinner in London began to 'resemble a game drive in the Masai Mara ... across the room there was a dress in zebra print and, grazing nearby, a zebra-striped handbag'. She noted that the fashion industry loves animal prints and rotates them for decades. Their appeal, she argues, is that

> Animal prints are a quotation, not just from the animal itself but from the primitive days when we wore animal skins, and – more recently – when wearing real fur was

Osa Johnson riding a zebra, photograph, 1921.

considered glamorous. Perhaps we have an atavistic urge to wear animals, a nostalgia for the days when we were hunters and they signified our dominance over nature and hence our survival.

The idea of animal prints, in this case zebra stripes, as a quotation is an appealing one, even if it is problematic to refer to a 'primitive' past. Zebra print, as discussed in our previous chapter, serves as shorthand for the exotic, the Other and the desire for nature. The frequency of zebra, and other animal, prints on the textiles that adorn human bodies reveals a complex attitude of admiration, domination, desire and longing that simultaneously draws attention to the absence of the *real* zebra. However, as Willis notes, animal print is 'so ubiquitous' these days that the effect is greatly diluted. Zebra, leopard and giraffe prints, among others, don't turn heads anymore: 'What nature designed to camouflage wild creatures in the dappled light of the African bush, we have tamed to blend in today.'[15]

There is, however, at least one context in which zebra stripes are sartorially unwelcome or controversial: the French Open. The Adidas Y-3 collection from 2016 created in collaboration with designer Yohji Yamamoto was, according to the company's press release, 'inspired by dazzle camouflage from the '40s and '50s'. Court attire consisting of headbands, visors, T-shirts, dresses, leggings and court shoes was printed with an array of monochrome zebra-like stripes. The design was intended to be visually arresting, and the language of the press release self-consciously adopted the language of the science of dazzle camouflage: 'the stripes in motion motif was not designed to conceal, but disrupt.'[16] The clothes worn by the tennis players Tomáš Berdych, Simona Halep, Ana Ivanović, Kristina Mladenović and Dominic Thiem, among others, certainly did cause disruption. A fashion editor at the *New York Times* wondered whether the 'eye-boggling black-and-white zebra stripes' might have affected play on the courts: 'It must be hard to keep an eye on the ball when faced with a riot of animal print.'[17] The kit print was described by some as 'hideous', 'eye-catching' and 'bizarre'. Others appraised the print in glowing terms. One social media user on Twitter, a fashion photographer, tweeted tennis player Ana Ivanović to tell her, 'You're the hottest zebra I know.'[18]

Paul Smith's idiosyncratic zebra, a veritable rainbow of colour, speaks to the theory of zebra stripes as individual markings that allow individual zebras to identify one another; likewise, we have seen how the fashion world continues to describe the purpose of the zebra's stripes as camouflage, disruptive – or even slimming (although vertical stripes, according to the Helmholtz illusion, actually make people look broader rather than slimmer). These are fairly widely held ideas about zebra stripes in popular culture, and until recently, scientists also presumed that predator evasion was the principle evolutionary pressure for the selection of stripes. A flurry of contemporary research has, however, started to look anew at zebra stripes and demonstrated that we must rethink the purpose of the zebra's stripes. Attempting to look at zebra stripes through the eyes of their predators has caused scientists to narrow down the search for the answer to the million-dollar question, why do zebras have stripes?

Tim Caro's *Zebra Stripes* (2016) is a systematic treatment of the theories of zebra striping, and a rebuttal of those that no longer stand the test of current field research. Caro, a professor of wildlife biology at the University of California (UC), Davis, is a specialist in animal coloration with extensive field experience. Broadly speaking, scientists have hypothesized that the evolutionary drive for stripes could be explained by one or more of the following:

147

- Crypsis (camouflage to avoid detection by predators).
- Aposematism (patternation to warn off predators).
- Dazzle (confusing predators when in flight).
- Intraspecific communication (a form of identification between zebras).
- Temperature regulation.
- Ectoparasite avoidance (diverting insects).

Recent experiments that have sought to reproduce zebras as seen by non-humans have proven that the long-held crypsis hypothesis does not stand up to scrutiny. A recent paper, 'Zebra Stripes Through the Eyes of Their Predators, Zebras, and Humans' (2016), by a team of researchers at the University of Calgary and UC Davis, describes the research that has sought to determine whether or not stripes render zebras cryptic to their large carnivore predators. Digital images of zebras were passed through filters that simulated species-specific visual systems – essentially an attempt to determine the maximum distances through which lions, spotted hyenas, humans and other zebras can resolve stripes. In daylight conditions, humans can resolve (identify and break up into constituent parts) zebra stripes at a distance 2.6 times the distance of zebras, 4.5 times the distance of lions and 7.5 times the distance of spotted hyenas. At dusk, when carnivores hunt, humans can see zebras from a distance greater than lions or spotted hyenas; lions can discern stripes at around 25–56 m (82–184 ft), hyenas at 15–34 m (49–112 ft). Beyond this distance, 'zebras bodies simply appear grey.' Thus, zebra stripes cannot serve as camouflage because they appear grey at a distance and, furthermore, are effectively useless once the predator is at a closer range (the range at which the predator resolves the stripes is easily within the range detection by scent or earshot). Amanda Melin et al. reason that stripes are unlikely to be a form of crypsis at far distances because predators would not be able to discern the black stripes against a treed background, or see white stripes blending in with bright shafts of light between trees (background matching).

So much for the Thayers' obliterative zebra cardboard cutouts positioned among grass and straw. In short, stripes cannot assist a zebra in blending into its surroundings until a predator is in close and dangerous proximity – 'distances at which predators could likely smell or hear zebras moving or breathing as they are particularly noisy herbivores'. A further consideration of the zebra's habitats and habits likewise puts to rest the probability of stripes evolving as cryptic camouflage. On open plains, all species are visible because of the contrast between their silhouette

Zebras scattered across grassland.

and the sky. There is no benefit to stripes in this context. Although stripes would, in theory, help a zebra blend into a wooded environment, this is not where zebras spend much of their time. Furthermore, as Melin et al. note, zebras create a lot of noise in woodland as they tread on twigs and branches. Even if a zebra were to stand perfectly still in a woodland habitat, it could be detected by scent alone. The distance at which camouflage comes into play is the distance at which a zebra can already be smelt out.[19]

It has been proposed that the black-and-white pelage, or hair, of the zebra might instead be aposematic: a warning, like the black-and-white markings of a skunk, or the bright coloration of a poison frog. Certainly, a zebra's bite and kick are formidable: they can even be fatal to a lion, but are frequently more effective against smaller predators. In general, however, zebras do not display much in the way of anti-predator behaviour like kicking or biting when faced with lions. Caro supposed that if zebras are an aposematic species, then they ought to show different responses and levels of vigilance towards predators like lions, hyenas and leopards, depending on whether they could reasonably tackle them.[20] In the field, Caro played these predators' sounds over speakers to different groups of zebras while feeding or drinking at a waterhole. Even the most vigilant zebra in a group spent less time looking in the direction of a hyena's whoop or leopard growl than in the direction of a lion's growl. He established that zebras do, in fact, 'find the presence of a hyena or leopard of less concern than a lion as judged by this measure of attentiveness'. Predator species are 'differentially threatening', so this might be linked to the relative sizes of predators and the zebra's advertised ability to defend itself – directed towards leopards, wild dogs and hyenas.[21] Caro's later research on the number and extent of wounds on zebras, giraffes, warthogs, impalas, waterbucks and other species does, however, cast doubt on a premature conclusion that zebras constitute an aposematic species. If zebras were such a species, then 'one might expect them to be attacked infrequently.'[22] Fieldwork conducted over three years suggests that they are not. Zebra wounds tended to be more severe than in other ungulates; fresh gashes are often deep enough to expose muscle, and might extend to up to 60 cm (24 in.) in length. The rate of wounding in observed zebras was around 8.1 per cent, much greater than in other species – 1.4 per cent of all observed impala, for example. If zebra pelage were truly aposematic, then we would expect them to be wounded *less* often than other species, not more.

The hypothesis that striped zebra pelage dazzles predators and makes it harder for carnivores to judge the speed and position of their moving prey has also come under increased scrutiny. Experiments conducted with human subjects attempting to 'capture' moving targets, and published in *Frontiers in Zoology* (2015), found that parallel-striped targets are 'significantly easier to capture' than perpendicular- and oblique-striped targets. The latter are also caught at the same rate as grey targets – not a promising finding for the idea that stripes dazzle captors; moreover, 'multiple striped targets are captured in fewer attempts and more quickly than grey targets.' This research was not specific to zebras; indeed, it could equally apply to striped butterfly fish or cichlids. It is also clear that not all stripes are created equal and have varying degrees of efficacy.[23] Caro, too, has found that stripes do not reduce predator-attack kill ratios. Data indicates that lions appear to target their zebra prey, and as established earlier, stripes are useless as dazzle in low-light conditions, when lions do much of their hunting. Caro compares the relative speeds of zebras and lions; a lion must catch a zebra within six seconds of revealing itself if it is to make a kill. A dazzle-induced confused state is unlikely as lions 'probably choose their victim before or

Zebras in the brush.

during the stalk before breaking cover'. Around 30 per cent of the annual mortality of zebras in the Serengeti can be attributed to lion predation. Moreover, lions actually have been shown in a long-term study in the Kruger National Park to kill a proportion of zebras greater than their relative abundance. Stripes are not, then, effective against lions – a zebra's greatest foe.[24]

It is fairly widely known that, similar to a human fingerprint, zebras have unique stripe patterns, and researchers use this to their advantage to identify individuals within a population. The Grévy's Zebra Trust, for example, regularly surveys and photographs zebras in the Wamba region, Kenya. The aim is to establish a database to provide information about zebra life histories, associated with photographs. In the 1960s the zoologists Hans and Ute Klingel took photographs of Grévy's zebras, constructed a bush darkroom to develop film and produced coded file-cards for each zebra. A coded system of identifying stripes enabled the Klingels to record zebras they had encountered before or observed for the first time. Today, stripe-identification software takes a photo of a zebra and can accurately identify it – like a barcode – even allowing for the distortion of stripes caused by pregnancy or thinning.[25] Stripes have also been hypothesized, by Jonathan Kingdon and others, as a means for zebras to identify conspecifics (members of their own species) and encourage allo-grooming (mutual grooming).[26] This idea is compelling, but runs into problems when we consider other equids. Equids have a large vocal repertoire and can also use the odour of dung to identify other individuals. Caro reasons that horses can identify individuals using visual signals 'without recourse to striped pelage', and other large herbivories without stripes successfully allogroom, bond and recognize one another.[27] Thus, although humans can,

Zebra running from a waterhole.

153

Hyena feasting upon a dismembered zebra head.

with patience and practice, identify individual zebras using stripes, it is difficult to determine the extent to which, if at all, zebras use stripes to identify conspecifics.

At this point only two remaining plausible hypotheses for why the zebra has its stripes remain: temperature regulation and ectoparasite avoidance. In 2015, a paper titled 'How the Zebra Got its Stripes: A Problem with Too Many Solutions' turned the focus on zebra striping towards thermoregulation. The authors of the study found that environmental factors such as temperature were a 'significant predictor of zebra stripe patterns across their entire range in Africa'.[28] Stripe thickness and definition on forelegs, hind legs and the torso are likely to be selected traits. Indeed, an infrared digital thermometer gun shows that zebras maintain a surface body temperature of 29.2°C (84.6°F), while similar-sized herbivores in similar conditions maintain a surface temperature of 32.5°C (90.5°F). Larison et al. suggest that while there is no clear support for the evolution of striping being driven by biting flies, the reduction of striping in areas with low seasonal temperatures could be a response to a reduction in the need for convective cooling, as well as a lower tsetse fly population; essentially, it is proposed that zebras in areas with cooler temperatures and fewer flies have reduced striping. Caro, on the other hand, does not consider there to be sufficient evidence to suggest that stripes aid in temperature reaction. His thermocamera data (infrared camera) did not produce any data that would suggest the surface temperature of a zebra is lower than that of an impala, buffalo or giraffe. In addition, since zebras often inhabit open plains with windy conditions, convection currents would do little to help cool an animal; likewise, any 'eddies over the animal's surface will dissipate as soon as the animal moves'.[29] For Caro, heat stress may be reduced by white stripes as a secondary consequence, but stripes are not an evolutionary response to heat stress itself.

The herd of zebra stripe hypotheses has now been reduced to a sole member: stripes as a defence against biting flies. Biting flies transmit a large number of dangerous or lethal diseases, including malaria, yellow fever, dengue, anthrax and equine infectious

A lion eats his recent kill.

anaemia virus, among others. Some flies have been discovered to have problems landing on striped surfaces, or to actively avoid them. It is thought that the different polarization of light from black-and-white surfaces disrupts the vision of polarotactic tabanids – flies like horseflies. Horseflies are irritating, interrupt grazing and carry disease. Promisingly, according to recent research carried out in Hungary, 'the light and dark stripes of a zebra's coat fall in a range where the striped pattern is most disruptive to tabanids.'[30] Experiments were carried out on both boards covered in insect glue in a field on a Hungarian horse farm, as well as on life-size 'sticky models'. Caro carried out field research in Africa and determined, too, that 'presence of body stripes is associated with tsetse fly distribution'.[31] In 2014, Caro carried out a series of experiments in Africa to explore in depth the relationship between striped pelage and ectoparasites. In one experiment, traps made of zebra and dark-brown wildebeest pelts were hung in the canopy around Lake Katavi, Tanzania; flies from a number of species were less likely to be found in the zebra pelt traps. Ectoparasite avoidance might well, then, be the principle force behind evolutionary selection of stripes. Ongoing research in this area is likely to make the promising correlation between zebra stripes and ectoparasites clearer. The problem of how the zebra got its stripes may have nearly been solved, or at least answers to that question have been substantially narrowed down; in the meantime, zebra stripes are posing a completely different kind of problem. The Quagga Project is attempting to get rid of zebra stripes.

The inspiration for the Quagga Project began when Reinhold Rau, a taxidermist at Cape Town's South Africa Museum, re-mounted a quagga foal and sent dried-tissue samples off for analysis. The quagga foal's hide still contained traces of muscle, tissue and blood vessels. Rau hoped that it might be possible to extract genetic information from these scant remains. Eventual genetic analysis of these samples in the 1980s, along with others, confirmed that the quagga was, in fact, a subspecies of the plains zebra. Quagga genes are, thus, diluted among the plains zebra population. It might then be possible, through selective breeding of plains zebras, to produce a quagga-like zebra. In 1987, nineteen wild plains zebras were selected for their reduced striping or any 'suggestion of a darker background colour'. There is significant colour variation in plains zebras, and there is, apparently, a 'gradient of progressive reduction in striping from north to south of their geographical distribution'. The quagga represents the 'extreme limit of the trend'. The zebras selected for the project were taken from areas within the quagga's original range, thus, in theory, selecting for plains zebras with some quagga traits or genes. The South African Museum provided accommodation and facilities, but funding had to be provided by grants, sponsorships and donations (in 2005 the project was transferred to the control of South African National Parks). The zoologist David Barnaby visited the project in the early 1990s and joined the project's founder, Reinhold Rau, on a reconnaissance trip to observe a newborn foal. This foal was said to be 'something of a disappointment', as it was less quagga-like than hoped. Rau called the herd of zebras over, 'Komm, Komm', and the herd approached him. Barnaby writes of the 'Rau magic' he experienced, the ease with which Rau was able to move in and out of the group photographing them – and in particular, their stripes – focusing particularly on the new foal. The foal, though 'not excessively Quagga-like', was 'not too disappointing either . . . it was a nice brown animal'. Reinhold generously named the foal after his visitor, and so it came to pass that a quagga-like male zebra came to be called 'David'.[32]

The Quagga Project's zebras are spread out across national parks and breeding locations. The Project's young, appealing foals with their light-brown colouring and reduced striping have, especially, garnered international media attention. After three generations, the effects of selective breeding could be seen; there had been a significant reduction in striping, whereas less progress had been made in background darkening.

In 2009, the Quagga Project was, however, confident that a quagga-like plains zebra could be produced in the fourth generation. This goal would be marked by 'achieving zero stripes on both the hindbody and legs'. These animals were to be released in a national park, in which plains zebras are absent. Eric Harley, a project leader and professor at Cape Town University, said that this would enable 'the visiting public to see a rendering of the zebra that the original occupants and settlers of the region would have encountered some hundreds of years ago, back in their original setting'.[33] As of 2016, the 4.5th generation of the quaggas began to show an increase in brown background colouring. According to another of the project's leaders, Mike Gregor, six of the project's one hundred animals are sufficiently quagga-like that they have now been given the new name 'Rau quaggas', in tribute to the founder Reinhold Rau. Once this number reaches fifty individuals, they will constitute a special herd of Rau quaggas with their own reserve. Critics of the Quagga Project point out that quaggas probably had genetic adaptations to the environment or behavioural characteristics that are different from plains zebras, that a quagga-like zebra is still a plains zebra. Its *quagganess* is superficial: taking stripes away from a zebra doesn't necessarily produce a quagga. The name 'Rau quaggas' seems to function as an acceptance of this criticism; however, Gregor, in an interview with CNN, said that it is better to try to remedy something than do nothing at all: 'If we can retrieve the animals or retrieve at least the appearance of the quagga, then we can say we've righted a wrong.'[34] In the same interview, Harley put the rationale for the project in similar terms: 'if we get animals which everybody agrees look like the quagga, then indeed we can say that the quagga was never really extinct.' Getting rid of stripes, then, seems to be an attempt to remove the stain of extinction from humanity's conscience. The 'Rau quagga' is as much a product of postcolonialism as it is a biological breakthrough.[35]

6 Z is for Zebra

Little known on the international stage just a few hundred years ago, zebras are now part of contemporary culture around the world. Regardless of their birthplace, most children today will recognize a zebra long before they have seen a live one, whether in a zoo or – more rarely – in the wild. African animals in particular have become a mainstay of children's books and toys. Present-day babies can relax in zebra bouncers, cuddle up to zebra soft toys and encounter anthropomorphized zebras in board books. Cute, large-headed zebras even have their own TV series in the form of *Zou*, a French-based animation based on the picture books of Michel Gay, which follows the everyday life of Zou, a young zebra who wears clothes and lives in a large house in the suburbs. For about U.S. $30 parents can buy their children a 'talking' soft toy called 'Robert the Zebra' programmed with twelve zebra facts including 'Hiya buddy! My name is Robert and I'm a zebra', 'The Safari Park is my home' and 'Do you like to run? I can run pretty fast: about 35 miles an hour [56 kph]'. At the higher end of the market, Prince George of Cambridge, third in line to the throne of Great Britain, is said to have received a hand-carved rocking zebra for Christmas in 2014, an object that retails at around £4,000. This special-edition rocking horse is very much marketed to the upper echelons of British society, to grace the kinds of homes that might already boast a taxidermy

Mabe, 'Z is for Zebra' from *The Animal Alphabet* (2013).

zebra head or two.[1] That a prince of Great Britain should ride a zebra rather than a horse speaks back to Walter Rothschild's zebra-drawn carriage ride to Buckingham Palace in the 1890s, and to Queen Charlotte's zebra housed in the Buckingham House paddock in the 1770s.

No self-respecting illustration of Noah's Ark, meanwhile, comes without a couple of zebras sunning themselves on the deck, often mingling with their natural enemies. The frequency with which zebras appear in children's literature might come down to two factors: first, their much-vaunted beauty and novelty; and second, the fact that they are the only well-known animal to begin with 'z' – if not the best-known 'z' word altogether. Compilers of children's alphabets flirt with zithers, zips, zoos and zucchini. More often than not, however, the zebra wins out.

One of the most famous alphabet-compilers, the British artist and poet Edward Lear (1812–1888), proved more imaginative than most.[2] 'Z was some zinc', for instance, eschews everyone's favourite black-and-white striped horse for a shiny piece of metal reflecting the 'sun's merry light'. But Lear couldn't resist the obvious every time. Zebras appear in several of his alphabets, with the rhyme usually a variation on the familiar story of the zebra's resistance to domesticity. A version from 1857, owned by the Yale Center for British Art, is relatively hopeful as regards the zebra's riding potential: 'Z was a Zebra / All striped white & black / And if he was tame / You might ride on his back / Z / Pretty old Zebra.' By 1880, however, in a version owned by the Victoria & Albert Museum, Lear strikes a slightly less confident tone: 'Z was a Zebra / All striped white & black / And he would not let any one / Ride on his back.' Though using the zebra to entertain children, Lear (a keen naturalist) obviously knew what sort of animal he was dealing with.

Lear's unmanageable zebra is categorized as male, as many zebra protagonists are, from Zou to Marty, the wise-cracking

Edward Lear, *Z was a Zebra*, 1857.

zebra from the *Madagascar* film franchise (2005–present). Despite this, zebras are still widely perceived as either appealing to female tastes or having 'feminine' qualities. The association between the zebra and female beauty, as noted in earlier chapters, is present in many African cultures. Just as wearing exotic animal skins has always tended to be the preserve of women in the Western world, so the zebra has been seen as an animal more likely to attract Western women than men. This may reflect its status as a smaller, more conspicuously elegant horse (although, of course, horses themselves have a reputation for being more admired by little girls than little boys). It might also reflect traditionally negative stereotypes of women as being beautiful but truculent – qualities that, as we have seen, are also regularly attributed to zebras (had Shakespeare lived a few hundred years later, perhaps we would have a play called *The Taming of the Zebra*).

There is certainly something of a tradition of the zebra perceived as a femme fatale, as seen through the examples of two particular female zebras, Jennie and Zelle. Jennie was a mountain zebra who came to London Zoo in 1907. She was described in a book from 1928 as a 'small zebra, with wicked eyes' and a changeable nature. Though perfectly well behaved in front of her keepers and the public, this 'dangerous and shrewish wife' was violent towards her 'three successive husbands' – note the shameless anthropomorphism – the first of which she 'deliberately kicked . . . to death'. Jennie eventually settled down with her third husband, Joe, who showed her who was 'master'.[3] Zelle, meanwhile, was a Grévy's zebra who lived at Seoul Zoo from 1984 to 2009. According to a South Korean newspaper, 'Zelle, who came to the zoo with three males, hogged all the attention from both visitors – and of course the male zebras – with her peculiar charm and graceful figure . . . Zelle especially drew interest after she killed all three males by kicking them.' After this, the femme fatale Zelle came to be given the nickname 'femme fa-mal' (a pun on *mal*, 말, the Korean word for horse; the Korean word for zebra is 얼룩말, *eollugmal*, literally 'striped horse').[4] This distinctly misogynistic language was picked up by another newspaper, which referred to Zelle's 'charming figure and haughty attitude', laying the blame on the zebra's seemingly cruel spirit, rather than on the zoo's failure to manage animals in captivity.[5] The name of the zebra, Zelle, referred to the original surname of the early twentieth-century Dutch dancer and convicted spy, Margaretha Macleod (also known as 'Mata Hari').

The idea of the zebra as an 'alternative' horse has clearly suited stories in which women take on roles usually confined to men. This is most evident in the character of Sheena, 'Queen of the Jungle', a comic-book character launched in 1937, and usually cited as not only the first ever female comic-book protagonist (pre-dating Wonder Woman by four years) but the first in a series of popular 'jungle girls' inspired by W. H. Hudson's novel *Green Mansions* (1904) and H. Rider Haggard's *She* (1886). Sheena starred in a successful series of Fiction House comic books before making a jump to the small screen in the 1950s, where she was played by the actress Irish McCalla (1928–2002) in *Sheena: Queen*

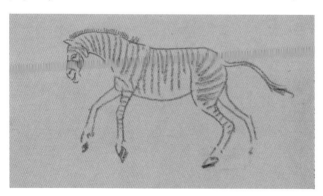

Gerrit Willem Dijsselhof, *Zebra*, c. 1904, graphite.

of the Jungle (1955–65). A big-screen adaptation followed in 1984, with Tanya Roberts in the lead role. Though widely derided, and something of a box-office failure, the film has since gathered a cult following.

The steamy opening credits of *Sheena* (1984) depict Roberts, as Sheena, riding across the hot African landscape (it was filmed in Kenya) on the back of her zebra Marika, accompanied by a synthesizer-heavy soundtrack. The sequence leaves us in no doubt that the main character, wearing the bare minimum of clothes, is being set up as an exotic and unconventional sex symbol. Sheena is the orphaned daughter of Western geologists, brought up by local tribespeople (the 'Zambouli'), who consider her their queen. She duly saves them from the threat posed by various outsiders, in what is a rather typical white person helps black people save themselves storyline – essentially the female equivalent of Tarzan. Sheena's trusty steed – in the film as in the original comic books – is a zebra, whom she has tamed and rides like a horse. Having grown up in Africa, Sheena is supposed to have a special talent for communicating with wild animals and, as a strong-minded and good-looking woman, could be said to be well placed to understand zebras in particular.

The story of a young, pretty woman breaking all the rules and riding on a zebra would return twenty years later, in a film aimed squarely at a children's audience. *Racing Stripes* (2005) concerns a young zebra (imaginatively named Stripes) who is left behind by a circus during a storm and rescued by an ex-racehorse trainer who owns a farm in Kentucky. The trainer acts on the advice of his teenage daughter, Chan, played by the actress Hayden Panettiere, and together they bring the animal up. Stripes is described by other animals as a 'funny looking horse' from the 'wrong side of the fence'. Much fun is made of the fact that he can't run as fast as a horse, which qualifies him as an inferior or pointless animal,

Sheena, Queen of the Jungle, first published in 1949 by Fiction House.

Zebras in
Chicago's Lincoln
Park Zoo (souvenir
postcard), 1909.

ZEBRA, LINCOLN PARK, CHICAGO

since the racetrack is 'the only reason for a horse to live'. Rather than dismiss this attitude out of hand, Stripes determines to beat the odds and become a racehorse. This he duly does, not without the help of his human friends, principally Chan who – like Sheena before her – is young, white, blonde, pretty and preternaturally good with animals. After a few inevitable setbacks, largely deriving from Stripes's overblown sense of his own capabilities, Chan eventually tames and rides Stripes to victory in a local derby (with added help from a Shetland pony, a goat, a pelican and two wise-cracking flies). He thus overcomes his difference by assimilating.

Racing Stripes plays with the idea that zebras should behave more like the rest of the horse species by introducing a zebra who actively wants to be a horse (sadly, no story we know of deals with a horse who wants to be a zebra). 'He wants to race, I can see it,' says one character; 'it's almost like he wants to be ridden,' says another. The film charts his struggles to be accepted as a horse, his acceptance that he is, in fact, a zebra, and his ability nonetheless to beat horses at their own game. It also gives credence to the idea that the best mount for a zebra is a woman. Chan is said to 'know' Stripes 'better than anyone ever could'. Their bond can be partly explained by the fact that both of them have lost their mothers; however, the film also seems to be drawing on the zebra's alternative status – different colouring, different size, different temperament – to explore ideas about gender, age and personal identity

Though set in Kentucky, *Racing Stripes* was filmed in South Africa, and took the challenge of riding zebras seriously. Working with several animals, experienced animal trainers and skilled film editors, they managed to create a relatively convincing case for the plausibility of zebra domestication. Interviews with the actors, nevertheless, suggest that the process was a difficult one. 'You've got your nice ones and you've got your horrible ones, and you've

Zebras in Forest Park Zoo, St Louis (souvenir postcard), 1920s–40s.

got your totally crazy ones,' Hayden Panettiere noted of her zebra co-stars: 'it's very different than riding a horse.'[6] Kicking and biting was common, and some Internet sources note that Panettiere suffered concussion and whiplash after being thrown from a zebra's back. The idea that a zebra could make a good racehorse, ultimately, fooled no one. As Panettiere pointed out, 'They're very slow animals actually, zebras. Very slow. Unless you stick a lion behind them and even then they won't even run in a straight line.'[7] This is probably something of an exaggeration – zebras have been known to run as fast as 55–65 kph (35–40 mph) – although it is true that they do so in a zigzag pattern.

The association between the alternative young woman and a zebra also appears, albeit more tangentially, in Wes Anderson's film *The Royal Tenenbaums* (2001). The character of Margot Tenenbaum, a stylish and moody literary genius who struggles to make the most of her early promise, is several times associated with zebras. As a child, she camps out in a natural history museum, sleeping below a taxidermy zebra. In her first play, performed on her eleventh birthday, she appears in a zebra costume. Her

Cover of *Jungle Comics*, no. 89 (1947).

bedroom, meanwhile, is decorated in a distinctive hand-printed wallpaper, featuring zebras being chased by arrows, which was produced by the designers Scalamandré and first used at Gino's Restaurant in New York in the 1930s.[8] Margot is clearly associated with many 'zebra-like' attributes: elegance, truculence and an enigmatic aloofness.

The 'not-a-horseness' (or 'not-quite-a-horseness') of the zebra remains integral to its reception. It is the wild form of something familiar, an animal whose coat not only combines seemingly opposing colours, but continues to stymie scientific analysis. You can see why the animal might appeal to teenagers. 'Zebra', the opening track of Baltimore dream-pop duo Beach House's popular album *Teen Dream* from 2010, appears to play off this appeal, as does the album's cover, a bleached representation of grazing zebras. The song itself is rich and mysterious: a tribute as much as a warning against the 'zebra' as the unknowable outsider. Whether the song is addressed to an actual zebra (as suggested by the chorus) or a zebra-like person is unclear. What does emerge clearly, however, is the image of the zebra being 'wild and wise'.

The zebra in this song, like Stripes in *Racing Stripes*, is a lone animal, much like the zebra in George Stubbs's painting and countless other images. It is the zebra removed from its natural context: that of the herd – an idea explored in the second film of DreamWorks' animated franchise *Madagascar* (2005–present). *Madagascar* follows a group of pampered zoo animals struggling to cope in the wild. Marty, a lively zebra voiced by the American comedian Chris Rock (catchphrase: 'crack-a-lackin') is a key character throughout the franchise, the improbably close friend of a lion called Alex. Marty has grown up in New York, away from other zebras, and does not encounter a zebra herd until they wind up in continental Africa (where exactly is never made clear) in the second film of the series. Upon encountering the herd, Marty discovers that – contrary to the reality of zebra herds – they are all physically identical, and that it is impossible to maintain a sense of individuality within it. The herd represents safety and a traditional sense of family, which by the end of the second film Marty decides to reject, preferring the company of other zoo animals. In one sense, then, the film seems to favour found communities over traditional family structures. This relatively positive message, however, is complicated by the fact that Marty's rejection of a zebra's natural habitat for a life of captive adventure in the West (first a zoo, later a travelling circus) comes with all sorts of negative connotations.

Life beyond the family herd is also a theme of the film *Khumba* (2013), another animated film aimed at children, which follows the adventures of a partially striped young zebra called Khumba,

Album cover of *Teen Dream* by the Baltimore band Beach House, released in 2010.

whose superstitious herd blames his unusual patterning for a drought (the implications of which are, of course, a continual threat for actual zebra populations). The film was made by a South African production company, and dedicated to Reinhold Rau, founder of the Quagga Project. The project returned the favour by naming one of their new foals Khumba, generating important publicity for both ventures. Despite the film's evident desire – and relative failure – to tap into the market created by *The Lion King* and *Madagascar, Khumba* has nonetheless been praised for recouping 'to some extent, the erasure of humanity' in its predecessors.[9] Khumba and his friends exist in an African landscape that bears at least some relationship to present-day reality, encountering, as they do, trucks of camera-wielding tourists, abandoned buildings and perimeter fences. Indigenous communities, however, remain absent. Though the film preaches tolerance, and certainly depicts zebras more faithfully than *Madagascar*, it is hampered by a convoluted and over-familiar plot.

Those seeking a more nuanced approach to the representation of animals in postcolonial Africa have to look beyond children's films, into the world of avant-garde Austrian film-making. Peter Kubelka's *Unsere Afrikareise* (Our Trip to Africa, 1966), a twelve-minute documentary detailing a hunting trip made by a group of Austrian tourists to Africa in 1961, has recently been described as 'one of the most powerful and insightful cinematic exposés of colonialism'.[10] The film started out as a commission, but Kubelka's relationship with his fellow travellers disintegrated during the journey, and he ended up using the footage for his own means, editing it into a disorientating collage in which violent scenes of big-game hunting are juxtaposed with Sudanese dancers and self-satisfied Europeans. The soundtrack for the film was recorded during the same trip, but is reordered so that sounds exist outside of their original context. Despite its brevity, the film lingers long

Zebras in San Diego Zoo (souvenir postcard).

in the memory. Among the many startling sequences are several glimpses of a wounded zebra thrashing on the ground and being skinned with a knife. We are reminded that there is much more to the zebra than its black-and-white pelage; under the skin is bright-red blood that runs in disorderly rivulets, spoiling the clean monochromatic lines.

When Kubelka made his film, criticism of colonial traditions such as big-game hunting was becoming increasingly widespread, and with it, a growing distaste for associated objects such as taxidermy trophies. The pith-helmet-wearing explorer was no longer seen as a heroic figure, but a pathetic throwback to the dark days of empire. However, while the killing of lions, giraffes and zebras still incites passionate debate – as exemplified by the controversy surrounding images of hunting posted online by Kendall Jones in 2014 and Aryanna Gourdin in 2016, and the killing of 'Cecil' the lion in 2015, among other incidents – taxidermy has undergone a surprising transformation from a dubious Victorian pastime to a hip, contemporary fashion. In the last few years,

Grévy's zebras in Akeley Hall diorama, American Museum of Natural History, New York.

interest in taxidermy has expanded greatly, spawning countless books and blogs.[11] Taxidermy shops such as Deyrolle in Paris, London Taxidermy and the Evolution Store in New York have all witnessed an upsurge in traffic, while many young people have been encouraged to try out taxidermy for themselves. Stag heads and stuffed squirrels have become a prerequisite for chic Brooklyn apartments and restaurants. Several companies even offer taxidermy rentals, for those whose dinner party is incomplete without a dead pelican or two. Aynhoe Park in Oxfordshire offers itself as a quirky wedding venue: one of its many eccentric attractions is a taxidermy zebra wearing a fez, mounted like a rocking horse.

There are many explanations for this present craze, ranging from the 'ironic' reappropriation of colonial imagery – now seen, rightly or wrongly, as being far enough in the past to have lost some of its potency – to the Internet's role as a giant community-created curiosity cabinet. Contemporary artists such as Polly Morgan, Kate Clark and Damien Hirst, whose works make consistent use of dead animals, have also had a large part to play. Morgan's work tends to feature smaller animals; however, the zebra has received the familiar formaldehyde treatment from Hirst. His work *The Incredible Journey* from 2008 features an adult zebra trapped in a glass box, seemingly encouraging viewers to make some connection between the long migration paths of zebras and the journey taken by this particular zebra post-death. The work sold at auction for just over £1 million – a price considered disappointing at the time (it was estimated to be at least double that).[12]

Despite the access contemporary audiences have to animals via zoos and nature documentaries, the closeness of the encounter afforded by taxidermy has undoubtedly helped it recover from its post-war unpopularity. Although series such as the BBC's *Africa* (2013) offer stunning imagery of zebras in their natural habitat, there is still a lot to be said for experiences such as the Akeley Hall of African Mammals at the American Museum of Natural History in New York, home of some of the most spectacular habitat dioramas ever created. Children growing up in New York today can see actual zebras at the Bronx Zoo, but they are unlikely to get as close as they can get to the taxidermy zebras in Akeley Hall. Zebras appear in three of the hall's 28 dioramas, designed by Carl Akeley in the 1920s and based directly on field observations. Plains zebras can be found grazing with Thomson's gazelles and eland in the Serengeti plains display, while Grévy's zebras join giraffes and oryxes at a Kenyan waterhole. Just in case the life of a zebra was made to look too easy, a zebra corpse (albeit a strangely bloodless one) appears in a display dedicated to jackals, vultures and hyena. Small children stop before each brightly lit case, occasionally turning to confirm with adults that what they are looking at isn't actually 'real'. Though the zebras have faded with time, more brown-and-yellow than black-and-white, the carefully constructed poses remain uncanny. These are not static or poorly mounted specimens, but meticulously crafted re-creations. An infant Grévy's zebra bends its neck to suckle at its mother's teat; the ears of a plains zebra twitch as if in anticipation of a nearby lion. For those unable or unwilling to go on a safari – a category into which most of us still fall – this feels closer to an authentic experience than seeing a zebra in a zoo, where animals have a knack for sleeping, hiding in corners or exhibiting behaviour that reminds us all too keenly that they are being held captive. On a trip to the Smithsonian National Zoo in Washington, DC, during the writing of this book, I stopped by the paddock where a lone male Grévy's zebra was kept. He was difficult to see through the wired fence, and was attracting little attention from visitors, most of whom were over

Plains zebras in the Akeley Hall diorama, American Museum of Natural History, New York.

at the panda enclosure, hoping for a sight of Bei Bei, the zoo's newest baby. Those who did stop to glance at the zebra couldn't help but note his rather conspicuous penis, which seemed an unwelcome distraction from the beauty of his striped coat. A light February drizzle fell on fresh dung. No one seemed to be enjoying themselves all that much.

The diorama, on the other hand, is nature nicely controlled; more tangible than nature on TV, but just as safe. A zebra in a zoo doesn't like being looked at all that much; these zebras, however, can hold your gaze all day. The animal that is most present in a habitat diorama is also the animal that is missing: humans. They shot, skinned and remounted these animals, carefully re-creating their environment with paint and plaster. No humans, however, appear in the dioramas themselves. Akeley Hall aims to present the 'biography of untouched Africa'.[13] Ironically, it takes many touches of the human hand to create this impression. As the diorama artist James Perry Anderson liked to say, the aim of his art is to conceal art. Museums are equally keen to conceal the role humans have taken in pushing animals like zebras to the brink of extinction, preferring to concentrate on the more hopeful role they are taking in conserving zebra habitats.

Of course, such conservation remains a complex issue. How do you keep a migratory animal contained within a national park? How do you balance the needs of local and international communities? How do you balance the economic benefits of the hunting industry against its cost? The money generated by allowing tourists to shoot zebras may yet ensure the survival of zebras, many argue. The zebra is no longer considered beautiful and useless; instead, its beauty *is* its use. Beauty attracts attention, generates revenue and demands preservation.

Certainly, the urge to hunt zebras shows no sign of slacking. If you're willing to pay $5,000 for the privilege, you can even hunt

Grévy's zebra in New York, souvenir postcard, c. 1910.

them on Texas ranches. If you'd rather just hang out with a zebra, foals can be readily purchased from about $3,000–$8,000 ('Give us a call to add this little cutie to you're herd' [*sic*] offers one website, next to a photograph of a bandy-legged foal).[14] Of course, for every person who thinks a zebra is cute, there is someone else who wants to take a selfie posing with a dead one, or eat a zebra burger (one of the leanest protein-heavy meats available on the market). These may even be the same people – such are the contradictions that surround most human relationships with animals.

The reality is that, for all the pop culture references (perhaps even because of them), most people are not even aware that one zebra species is listed as endangered and that the other two are considered vulnerable or near threatened. The question that most people seem most concerned about is whether they are black with white stripes or white with black stripes (it's the former, as noted earlier). The idea of the 'zebra' has travelled far beyond the

180

actual animal, as this book has hoped to show, accruing a range of meanings. Kids who love Marty the zebra don't much mind that he does not behave remotely like a zebra; a man or woman wearing zebra print may not stop to think about the animal that inspired it; and the dream of riding a zebra will no doubt continue to fly in the face of all the evidence. The loss of the quagga doesn't keep many people up at night, though it is no doubt considered 'neat' that someone should be making Herculean efforts to resurrect it. Such is the way we are with animals. They lure us in, but we can only go so far. So we fill in the gaps, and they get wrapped up in our own needs and desires. They get used and abused, distorted and displaced. We look at the zebra, and the zebra looks back, but our knowledge about the zebra has its epistemological

Samuel Jessurun de Mesquita, *Zebra, from behind*, early 20th century, paper and chalk.

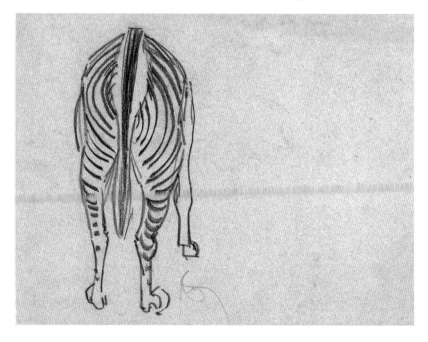

limits. What is it like to be a zebra? Certainly, the life cycle and biology of zebras is well described, but this stops short of answering the question. The zebra's striped hide is like a broad canvas upon which human cultures, past and present, have painted meaning. The zebra is a metaphor, a symbol, something to think with. Z may be for zebra, but all we are left with in the end is ourselves.

Timeline of the Zebra

3.5 MYA	20,000–28,000 YA	1ST–2ND CENTURIES AD	6TH CENTURY

Presumed dating of the Hagerman Horse (*Equus simplicidens*), discovered in 1928 in Hagerman, Idaho, and considered to have been closer in kind to a Grévy's zebra than to any modern horse

Earliest estimated dating of southern African rock art, in which zebras occasionally appear

Zebras appear in Roman games

Zebras appear in Byzantine mosaics

1621	1763	1777–86	1783

Ustad Mansur presents a zebra painting to the Mughal Court

George Stubbs paints Queen Charlotte's mountain zebra, one of the first zebras to be seen in England

Robert Jacob Gordon travels into the southern African interior, and becomes the first Westerner to make painted records of zebras in their natural habitat

The French state begins a three-year quest to acquire two zebras for the Royal Menagerie

1883	1890s		1937

Last known quagga dies in captivity at Artis Royal Zoo in Amsterdam

Walter Rothschild rides a zebra-drawn carriage through London; a British journal publishes an article on the 'Downfall of the Zebra', prophesizing imminent extinction

Foundation of Mountain Zebra National Park outside Cradock in the Eastern Cape. Numbers of Cape Mountain zebras are thought to have dropped as low as 100 prior to this

| 1000–1500 | 12TH–13TH CENTURIES | 1417 | 1591 |

The Shona construct the stone city of Great Zimbabwe, population 10,000–20,000. Zebra stripes, figures and other representations reveal the importance of the zebra in the Shona belief system

Zebras are exchanged as diplomatic gifts across the Islamic world

The Chinese Emperor Yong-Le receives a zebra as a gift from Somalia

Italian explorer Filippo Pigafetta records impressions of the zebra after a trip to central Africa, and suggests that they could be domesticated

| 1795–1820 | 1840 | 1863–70 | 1882 |

Following the seizure of Cape Colony by the British from the Dutch in 1795, which forces Dutch settlers into the interior, and causes friction with indigenous communities, major accounts of the region and its animals are published by William Burchell, Samuel Daniell and others

William Cornwallis Harris, father of big-game hunting, publishes *Portraits of the Game and Wild Animals of Southern Africa*, containing several images of zebras

The only surviving photographs of a quagga are taken from an animal owned by London Zoo

Grévy's zebras acquire their name, taken from French President Jules Grévy, courtesy of the French naturalist Émile Oustalet

| 1951 | 2012 | 2016 | 2017 |

Serengeti National Park in Tanzania, now home to the largest population of plains zebra in the world, is founded

A scientific study published in *Oryx* reveals that the migration of the plains zebra is the 'longest of all known mammal migrations in Africa'. Birth of Khumba, Quagga Project foal

Comprehensive new scientific study narrows down possible causes of striping in zebras

Two of the three zebra species (mountain and Grévy's) remain 'vulnerable' and 'endangered'

References

INTRODUCTION: DEFINING THE ZEBRA

1 Thomas Pennant, *History of Quadrupeds* (London, 1781), vol. I,
   pp. 13–14.
2 William Burchell, *Travels in the Interior of Southern Africa*
   (London, 1822), vol. II, p. 225.
3 Marina Cano, 'Beauty and the Beast', *Popular Photography*
   (April 2008), p. 65.
4 Dorcas MacClintock, *A Natural History of Zebras* (New York, 1976),
   pp. 3–4, and R. Lydekker, *The Horse and its Relatives* (London, 1912),
   pp. 187–8. Other sources suggest words of Congolese or Amharic
   origin – or a bastardization of the Latin *equiferus* (meaning 'fierce
   horse').
5 Jonathan Kingdon, *East African Mammals* (London, 1979), vol. III,
   pp. 143, 179.
6 Simon Hattenstone, 'Going Underground: Meet the Man who
   Lived as an Animal', *The Guardian* (23 January 2016),
   www.theguardian.com.
7 See, for instance, the well-publicized apartment of New York
   designer Ryan Korban, which features both a taxidermy zebra
   and a zebra-skin rug.
8 The Reverend John Kidgell, *Original Fables* (London, 1763), p. 77.
9 David Willoughby, *The Empire of Equus* (New York, 1974), p. 334.
10 MacClintock, *A Natural History*, pp. 10–13.
11 Filippo Pigafetta, *A Report of the Kingdome of Congo, a Region of
   Africa and of the Countries that Border Rounde about the Same*,

trans. Abraham Hartwell (London, 1597), pp. 50–51. Thanks to Roy Booth's blog Early Modern Whale for the reference.

12 Anon, 'Racehorse Owner Earns his Stripes by Learning to Ride a Zebra . . . The Animal that Cannot Be Tamed', *Daily Mail* (4 June 2009), www.dailymail.co.uk.

13 Despite the fact that there is a historical precedent for breaking in zebras, such reports usually claim that said rider is the 'first' to 'tame the untameable'. Horseman Gary Witheford, for instance, who seems to have trained as many as four zebras, claims on his website that he is 'the first man to break in zebras', a claim for which there is zero evidence. See www.garywitheford.co.uk, accessed 2 August 2017.

14 Alexandre Jardin, *Le Zèbre* (Paris, 1988). See also www.bleublanczebre.fr.

15 Tim Caro, *Zebra Stripes* (Chicago, IL, 2016), p. 21.

16 Jonathan Kingdon, *Mammals of Africa* (London, 2013), vol. V, p. 417.

17 See C. P. Groves and Catherine H. Bell, 'New Investigations on the Taxonomy of the Zebras Genus *Equus*, Subgenus *Hippotigris*', *Mammalian Biology*, vol. LXIX (2004), pp. 182–96.

18 Willoughby, *Empire of Equus*, p. 354. See Groves and Bell, 'New Investigations', for further discussion of different names.

19 For more on current debates surrounding equid evolution, see Caro, *Zebra Stripes*, pp. 8–12.

20 For a more detailed description of a zebra's biological history, see the following studies: Kingdon, *Mammals of Africa*; Willoughby, *Empire of Equus*; MacClintock, *A Natural History*; and Caro, *Zebra Stripes*.

21 Willoughby, *Empire of Equus*, p. 334.

22 Kingdon, *Mammals of Africa*, p. 419.

23 Ibid., p. 420.

24 MacClintock, *A Natural History*, p. 55.

25 See Caro, *Zebra Stripes*, p. 20.

26 Tim and Rosie Holmes, in correspondence with the author.

27 See Groves and Bell, 'New Investigations', pp. 182–96.

28 For example, Caro, *Zebra Stripes*, p. 12. Caro refers to five subspecies: the quagga, Grant's zebra, Crawshay's zebra, Chapman's zebra and the 'Upper Zambezi species'.

29 Ibid., p. 182.

30 R. Naidoo et al., 'A Newly Discovered Wildlife Migration in Namibia and Botswana is the Longest in Africa', *Oryx*, v/1 (2016), pp. 138–46.

31 Tim and Rosie Holmes, in correspondence with the author.

32 The zoologist Alphonse Milne-Edwards is sometimes credited with the naming instead.

1 ZEBRAS AT HOME

1 Brenda Sullivan, *Spirit of the Rocks* (Cape Town, 1995), p. 50. Chris Peers, *Warrior Peoples of East Africa, 1840–1900* (Oxford, 2005), p. 8.

2 Ibid.

3 Megan Biesele, *Women Like Meat: The Folklore and Foraging Ideology of the Kalahari Ju/'hoan* (Bloomington, IN, 1993), p. 116.

4 Olubandele Dada, *West African Folk Tales* (Pittsburgh, PA, 1970), pp. 9–10.

5 Penny Miller, *Myths and Legends of Southern Africa* (Cape Town, 1979), p. 29.

6 Claudine Renaud, 'SA Tightens Surrogacy Guidelines', *Independent Online* (13 October 2011), www.iol.co.za.

7 John Berger, 'Why Look at Animals?', in *About Looking* (New York, 1980), pp. 3–28.

8 Aaron Hodza and George Fortune, eds, *Shona Praise Poetry* (Oxford, 1979), p. 175.

9 Elizabeth MacGonagle, *Crafting Identity in Zimbabwe and Mozambique* (Rochester, NY, 2007), p. 56.

10 Thomas Huffman, *Snakes and Crocodiles: Power and Symbolism in Ancient Zimbabwe* (Johannesburg, 1996), pp. 100, 149.

11 Roselyn Sachiti, 'Man "Co-habits" with Zebra', *The Herald* (21 February 2014), www.herald.co.zw.

12 Loirdham Moyo, 'Dorothy Mabika: I Turned Down Mutasa's Sexual Advances', *Voice of America Zimbabwe* (9 May 2013), www.voazimbabwe.com.

13 Brian Raftopoulos and Tyrone Savage, eds, *Zimbabwe: Injustice and Political Reconciliation* (Cape Town, 2004), p. 277.

14 Mary J. Maher, *Racism and Cultural Diversity* (London, 2012), p. 233.

15 Lawrence Hill, 'Zebra: Growing Up Black and White in Canada', in *Talking About Identity: Encounters in Race, Ethnicity, and Language*, ed. C. James and A. Shodd (Toronto, 2001), pp. 44–50.

16 Franz Fanon, *Black Skins, White Masks* (New York, 1967).

17 George Elliott Clarke, *Odysseys Home: Mapping African-Canadian Literature* (Toronto, 2002), p. 227.

18 Jonathan Capehart, 'What Do a Zonkey and Obama Have in Common?', *Washington Post* (30 April 2014), www.washingtonpost.com.

19 Mychal Denzel Smith, 'What Chris Rock Meant by President Obama's "Whiteness"', *The Guardian* (8 June 2012), www.theguardian.com; Andrew Kirell, 'Chris Rock on Playing Zebra in *Madagascar 3*: "In Honor of Our Zebra President"' (7 June 2012), www.medialite.com.

20 David Gillota, *Ethnic Humor in Multiethnic America* (London, 2013), pp. 115–17.

21 Ibid.; *Madagascar: Escape 2 Africa* [script], www.script-o-rama.com.

2 ZEBRAS ON THE MOVE

1 Quoted in Som Prakash Verma, *Mughal Painter of Flora and Fauna, Ustad Mansur* (New Delhi, 1999), p. 41.

2 D. Osborn and J. Osbornovà, *The Mammals of Ancient Egypt* (Warminster, 1998).

3 Kenneth Kitchell, *Animals in the Ancient World from A to Z* (London, 2010), p. 204. Mary Beagon, 'Wondrous Animals in Classical Antiquity', in *The Oxford Handbook of Animals in Classical Thought and Life*, ed. Gordon Lindsay Campbell (Oxford, 2014),

pp. 414–40. D'Arcy Thompson, 'The Greek for a Zebra', *Classical Review*, LVII (1943), pp. 103–4.

4 Archaeologists have also noted that the giraffe, rather squished and resembling something of a camel, could not have been seen by the artist in life.

5 John Peters, Hermann Thiersch and Stanley Cook, *Painted Tombs in the Necropolis of Marissa* (London, 1905), p. 93.

6 George Jennison, *Animals for Show and Pleasure in Ancient Rome* (Manchester, 1937), p. 89.

7 Jocelyn Toynbee, *Animals in Roman Life and Art* (Baltimore, MD, 1996), p. 167. Linda Kalof, ed., *A Cultural History of Animals in Antiquity* (Oxford, 2011).

8 Rachel Hachlili, *Ancient Mosaic Pavements: Themes, Issues, and Trends* (Boston, MA, 2009). Diklah Zohar, 'A New Approach to the Problem of Pattern Books in Early Byzantine Mosaics: The Depiction of the Giraffe in the Near East as a Case Study', *Early Christian Art*, V (2008), pp. 123–46.

9 Timotheus' description of the two giraffes at Gaza can be found in Remke Kruk, 'Encounters with the Giraffe, from Paris to the Medieval Islamic World', in *Classical Arabic Humanities in Their Own Terms*, ed. Beatrice Gruendler and Michael Cooperson (Boston, MA, 2008), pp. 569–92.

10 A. Moule, 'Some Foreign Birds and Beasts in Chinese books', *Journal of the Royal Asiatic Society of Great Britain and Ireland*, 2 (1925), pp. 247–61.

11 J. Duyvendak, 'The True Dates of the Chinese Maritime Expeditions in the Early Fifteenth Century', *T'oung Pao*, 34 (1939), pp. 341–413. Samuel Wilson, *The Emperor's Giraffe and Other Stories of Cultures in Contact* (Boulder, CO, 1999), p. 125.

12 Neil MacGregor, *A History of the World in 100 Objects* (London, 2012).

13 Sushil Chaudhury and Kéram Kévonian, eds, *Armenians in Asian Trade in the Early Modern Era* (Delhi, 2014), p. 327.

14 William Ridgeway, *The Origin and Influence of the Thoroughbred Horse* (Cambridge, 1905), p. 125.

15 Doris Behrens-Abouseif, *Practicing Diplomacy in the Mamluk Sultanate: Gifts and Material Culture* (London, 2014), p. 327.

16 Shelby Thacker and José Escobar, *Chronicle of Alfonso x* (Lexington, KY, 2002), p. 47.

17 Joseph O'Callaghan, *Alfonso x and the Cantigas de Santa María: A Poetic Biography* (Boston, MA, 1998), p. 95.

18 Behrens-Abouseif, *Practicing Diplomacy in the Mamluk Sultanate*, Chapter Three.

19 Andreu Martínez d'Alòs-Moner, *Envoys of a Human God: The Jesuit Mission to Christian Ethiopia, 1557–1632* (Boston, MA, 2015), p. 73.

20 Som Prakash Verma, *Mughal Painter of Flora and Fauna, Ustad Mansur* (New Delhi, 1999), p. 41. Asok Kumar Das, *Wonders of Nature: Ustad Mansur at the Mughal Court* (Mumbai, 2013), pp. 12–23.

21 The zebra depicted by Mansur was not the only one to come to the Mughal Court in the seventeenth century; other paintings made in the same period and after show different species of zebra, including one given to Emperor Aurangzeb in 1665.

22 Duarte Lopes and Filippo Pigafetta, *A Report of the Kingdom of Congo* (London, 1881), p. 51.

23 Georges-Louis Leclerc, Comte de Buffon, *Barr's Buffon: Buffon's Natural History* (London, 1797), p. 90.

24 Robbins pieced together this quest for a zebra from a chain of letters between officials and captains. See Louise Robbins, *Elephant Slaves and Pampered Parrots: Exotic Animals in Eighteenth-century Paris* (Baltimore, MD, 2002), pp. 52–60.

25 Ibid.

26 David Barnaby, *Quaggas and Other Zebras* (Plymouth, 1996), p. 66.

27 Caroline Grigson, *Menagerie: The History of Exotic Animals in England* (Oxford, 2016), p. 165.

28 Christopher Plumb, *The Georgian Menagerie: Exotic Animals in Eighteenth-century London* (London, 2015), pp. 185–94.

29 William Mason to Horace Walpole, 2 June 1773, in Warren Hunting Smith and George Lam, *Horace Walpole's Correspondence, 1756–1799* (New Haven, CT, 1955), pp. 90–91.

30 Christopher Plumb, "'The Queen's Ass': The Cultural Life of Queen Charlotte's Zebra in Georgian Britain', in *The Afterlife of Animals*, ed. Samuel Alberti (Charlottesville, VA, 2011), pp. 17–36.

31 Stephen Eisenman, *The Cry of Nature* (London, 2013), p. 110.

32 Alec Guinness, *My Name Escapes Me: The Diary of a Retiring Actor* (London, 1997) , p. 171.

33 Samuel Ward, *A Modern System of Natural History* (London, 1775), p. 81.

34 John Bigland, *Letters on Natural History* (London, 1806), p. 70.

35 Plumb, *The Georgian Menagerie*, pp. 185–94.

3 COLONIZING THE ZEBRA

1 There are claims that quaggas may have existed, in very small numbers, well into the twentieth century. This is not impossible, though it does not change the fact that most quaggas were extinct well before then. See Attilio Gatti, *Here is the Veld* (New York, 1948) and Peter Heywood, 'The Quagga and Science: What Does the Future Hold for this Extinct Zebra?', *Perspectives in Biology and Medicine*, LVI/1 (2013), pp. 54–5.

2 Vernon S. Forbes, *Pioneer Travellers of South Africa: A Geographical Commentary Upon Routes, Records, Observations and Opinions of Travellers at the Cape, 1750–1800* (Cape Town, 1965) and L. C. Rookmaaker, *The Zoological Exploration of South Africa, 1659–1790* (Rotterdam, 1989).

3 Anders Sparrman, *A Voyage to the Cape of Good Hope, Towards the Antarctic Polar Circle, and Round the World: But chiefly into the Country of the Hottentots and Caffres, from the Year 1772 to 1776* (London, 1785).

4 Ibid., p. 130.

5 Ibid., pp. 224–7.

6 Ibid.

7 John Barrow, *An Account of Travels into the Interior of Southern Africa, in the Years 1797 and 1798* (London, 1806), p. 44.

8 Sparrman, *A Voyage*, p. 224.

9 William Paterson, *A Narrative of Four Journeys into the Country of the Hottentots and Caffraria in the Years 1777, 1778, 1779* (London, 1790), p. 76.

10 Robert Jacob Gordon, *Cape Travels, 1777 to 1786* (Johannesburg, 1988), vol II, p. 387.

11 Paterson, *A Narrative*, p. 119.

12 Jacob Gordon, *Cape Travels*, p. 273.

13 Ibid., p. 281.

14 Ibid.

15 The exception to this rule is the quagga foal, which Gordon managed to separate from a large herd and kept for a day before releasing her. See P. Tuijn, 'Historical Notes on the Quagga', *Bijdragen Tot de Dierkunde*, XXXVI (1966), pp. 75–9.

16 As Tuijn notes, Gordon's images were frequently recycled, later appearing in Dutch editions of Buffon's *Histoire Naturelle*, ibid.

17 Captain Robert Percival, *An Account of the Cape of Good Hope* (London, 1804), p. 93.

18 Ibid., pp. 121, 162.

19 Katherine Prior, *An Illustrated Journey Round the World by Thomas, William and Samuel Daniell* (London, 2007).

20 For a good history of early images of the quagga, see Dolores M. Gall, '"This Most Elegant of Quadrupeds" – Illustrations of the Quagga', *Discovery*, XV/2 (1980–81), pp. 44–51.

21 Edna and Frank Bradlow, eds, *William Somerville's Narrative of his Journey to the Eastern Cape Frontier and to Lattakoe, 1799–1802* (Cape Town, 1979), pp. 35–6.

22 Ibid.

23 Ibid., p. 68.

24 See Roger Stewart and Brian Warner, 'William John Burchell: The Multi-skilled polymath', *South African Journal of Science*, CVIII (2012), pp. 1–9.

25 He expressed this wish in a letter to his mother, written in May 1811: see W. J. Burchell, *Travels in the Interior of Southern Africa* (London, 1953), vol. II, p. 424.

26 Burchell, *Travels in the Interior*, vol. I, p. 173. Zebras are mentioned frequently in Burchell's writings, though rarely at length. See vol. I, p. 101, for a discussion of differences between mountain and plains zebras.

27 For the origin of this much-repeated story, see Edward B. Poulton, *William John Burchell: The Materials of a Lecture Delivered before the British Association in the Town Hall, Cape Town, Aug. 17, 1905* (London, 1907).

28 For more on Harris and his hunting contemporaries, see Jane Carruthers, 'Changing Perspectives on Wildlife in Southern Africa', *Society and Animals*, XIII/3 (2005), pp. 183–200.

29 William Cornwallis Harris, *The Wild Sports of Southern Africa: Being the Narrative of a Hunting Expedition from the Cape of Good Hope, through the Territories of the Chief Moselekatse, to the Tropic of Capricorn* (London, 1852), p. xiii.

30 This was more recently reprinted with an introductory essay and additional illustrations: William Cornwallis Harris, *Portraits of the Game and Wild Animals of Southern Africa* (Cape Town, 1969).

31 Cornwallis Harris, *Portraits of the Game*, p. 152.

32 Ibid., p. 11.

33 Ibid., p. 28.

34 Anon, 'Hunting the Zebra', *Parley's Magazine*, V (1837), p. 336.

35 Reinagle's *Landscape with Animals (an African Scene)*, 1828, is owned by Doncaster Museum and Art Gallery.

36 Earl of Morton, 'A Communication of a Singular Fact in Natural History', *Philosophical Transactions of the Royal Society of London*, III (1821), pp. 20–22. For further commentary, see Jim Endersby, *A Guinea Pig's History of Biology* (Cambridge, 2009) and Heywood, 'The Quagga and Science', pp. 53–64.

37 The original poem is six verses long. H. G. Adams, 'Lines on Rarey's Zebra', in *The Ladies Cabinet of Fashion* (undated [c. 1858]), p. 238. See also Anon., 'The Horse-tamer and the Zebra', *The Lady's Newspaper* (29 May 1858), p. 343.

38 *Illustrated Times* (10 July 1858), pp. 17–18.

39 For more on the society, see Christopher Lever, *They Dined on Eland: The Story of the Acclimatization Societies* (London, 1992).

40 *Punch's Almanack for 1865* (London, 1865).

41 *Punch* (24 July 1858), p. 40.

42 Wilfrid Blunt, *The Ark in the Park: The Zoo in the Nineteenth Century* (London, 1976), p. 40.

43 Eight mounted zebra can be found on display at Tring today. For discussion of these, see Rachel Poliquin, *The Breathless Zoo* (Philadelphia, PA, 2012), pp. 111–13.

44 Miriam Rothschild, *Walter Rothschild: The Man, The Museum and the Menageries* (London, 2008), pp. 108–9.

45 H. A. Bryden, 'Zebras and their Characteristics', *Pall Mall Magazine* (July 1896), p. 384.

46 See David Barnaby, ed., *Letters to Mr Tegetmeier from J. Cossar Ewart and Others to the Editor of The Field at the Turn of the Nineteenth Century* (Timperly, 2004).

47 See, for example, 'Possibilities of the Zebra', *The Speaker*, 26 August 1905), pp. 206–7.

48 As noted above, most colonizers didn't take to zebra meat, though Africans continued to eat it. As Dorcas MacClintock has noted, the Dutch used quagga skins as grain bags, sacks and footwear. Dorcas MacClintock, 'Professor Marsh's Quagga Mare', *Discovery*, xv/2 (1980–81), pp. 35–9.

49 Evidently the writer's national identity demands that the blame for the animal's demise be laid everywhere but the feet of the British colonists. 'The Downfall of the Zebra', *All the Year Round* (19 April 1890), pp. 375–8.

50 Laurence Irwell, 'About Zebras', *The Western Field* (1907), pp. 826–35.

51 Carruthers, 'Changing Perspectives on Wildlife in Southern Africa', p. 194.

52 See MacClintock, 'Professor Marsh's Quagga Mare', pp. 35–9.

1 The company has also sponsored football teams (including Tottenham Hotspur in cup competitions from 2010 to 2013) and rugby tournaments.

2 *Private Insight* (Summer 2011), see www.investec.co.uk for more information.

3 See www.zebrapen.co.uk/company-profile, accessed 2 August 2017. There are countless other companies that use zebras somewhere in their name or in their marketing.

4 Advertised on eBay at the time of writing.

5 'Zebra Hides and Rugs', Rojé Exotics, www.rojeleather.com, accessed 23 September 2016.

6 Chris Nichols, *The Leisure Architecture of Wayne McAllister* (Layton, UT, 2007).

7 This phrase was used on the back of the postcard reproduced in this chapter.

8 According to a recent study, Hearst began collecting animals in 1924; he seems to have owned at least five zebras by 1927. See Maria Belozerskaya, *The Medici Giraffe and Other Tales of Exotic Animals and Power* (New York, 2006), pp. 339–41.

9 For instance, Gene Lees, *Cats of Any Color: Jazz Black and White* (Boston, MA, 2009), p. 53.

10 See online catalogue at www.vam.ac.uk.

11 See 'animal print' entry in Valerie Steele, *Encylopedia of Clothing and Fashion* (New York, 2005).

12 *Jungle Comics No. 18* (June 1941).

13 See www.robertgiardfoundation.org/galleries/nudes, accessed 2 August 2017.

14 Cath Clarke, 'Lucian Freud's Feathered Friend', *The Guardian* (16 June 2010), www.theguardian.com.

15 Mary Fedden, 'Mary Fedden: An Artist's Diary', *Art Review*, vol. XLVII (1995), pp. 44–5.

16 Mel Gooding, *Mary Fedden* (Aldershot, 1995), pp. 7, 38.

17 Brian Foss, *War Paint: Art, War, State, and Identity in Britain, 1939–45* (New Haven, CT, 2007), p. 41.

18 Angela Weight, *Carel Weight: A War Retrospective* (London, 1995), p. 11.

19 Quoted in Jane Clark, *Sidney Nolan: Landscapes and Legends* (National Gallery of Victoria, 1987), p. 144.

20 Quoted in Dorcas MacClintock, *A Natural History of Zebras* (New York, 1976), p. 27.

21 The work is owned by the New South Wales Gallery. Ian North kindly shared his thoughts on the painting in person, from which I quote here.

22 David Rimanelli, 'Michael Joo', *Artforum International*, XLVIII/6 (February 2010), p. 198.

23 Rory Carnegie, *Long Ago and Far Away* (London, 2016).

24 See Daniel Naudé, *Animal Farm* (London, 2012).

5 STRIPES

1 Gladys Davidson, *At Whipsnade Zoo* (London, 1934), pp. 64–6.

2 Alfred Wallace, *Darwinism: An Exposition of the Theory of Natural Selection* (London, 1889), p. 220.

3 Gerald Thayer, *Concealing-coloration in the Animal Kingdom* (New York, 1909), pp. 261–71.

4 Hugh Murphy and Martin Bellamy, 'The Dazzling Zoologist: John Graham Kerr and the Early Development of Ship Camouflage', *The Northern Mariner/Le Marin du nord*, 19 (2009), pp. 171–92.

5 *Punch Magazine* (7 April 1915), p. 280.

6 Henry Conroy, *Callaghan* (London, 2006), p. 22.

7 George Charlesworth, *A History of the Transport and Road Research Laboratory* (Aldershot, 1987), p. 108.

8 'The Abbey Road Zebra Crossing Is "Listed" by Tourism and Heritage Minister John Penrose', Department for Culture, Media and Sport (22 December 2010), www.gov.uk.

9 Jon Henley, 'End of the Road for the Zebra?', *The Guardian* (31 October 2011), www.guardian.com.

10 'African Flying Safari 1933', Safari Museum, www.safarimuseum. com, accessed 29 September 2016.

11 Patrick Clark, 'Interview: Adam Lambert', *Schön!* (30 September 2015), http://schonmagazine.com.

12 Comments by Instagram users on Adam Lambert's Instagram account (_sehrkreativername_, kylieeeeeeeeeeeeeee, and cmariena333, respectively).

13 Paul Smith, *Paul Smith: A to Z* (New York, 2012).

14 The title of Smith's book is *A to Z*; it chronicles his life and interests, from 'Abbey Road' to 'Zebra'.

15 Rebecca Willis, 'Animal Prints Are Now So Familiar that They Don't Roar their Message. But They Still Have Plenty to Say', *The Economist: 1843 Magazine* (January 2013), www.1843magazine.com.

16 'Adidas Tennis and Y-3 set to rock Roland Garros with a Standout Collection' [press release], Adidas (2 April 2016), http://news.adidas.com.

17 Vanessa Friedman, 'At the French Open, Adidas Courts Controversy with Camouflage', *New York Times* (27 May 2016), www.nytimes.com.

18 Spiro Mandylor (@itsallstyletome), 'Congrats@Analvanovic! You're the hottest zebra I know', Twitter (07.37, 24 May 2016), www.twitter.com.

19 Amanda Melin, Donald Kline, Chihiro Hiramatsu and Tim Caro, 'Zebra Stripes Through the Eyes of their Predators, Zebras, and Humans', *PLOS ONE*, XI/3 (22 January 2016), http://journals.plos.org.

20 Tim Caro, *Zebra Stripes* (Chicago, IL, 2016), p. 63.

21 Ibid., p. 64.

22 Ibid., p. 66.

23 Anna Hughes, Richard Magor-Elliott and Martin Stevens, 'The Role of Stripe Orientation in Target Capture Success', *Frontiers in Zoology*, XII/3 (2015).

24 Caro, *Zebra Stripes*, p. 92.

25 'Stripe Recognition', Grevy's Zebra Trust, www.grevyszebratrust.org, accessed 11 September 2016.

26 Jonathan Kingdon, *East African Mammals*, vol. III (London, 1979), pp. 130–38.

27 Caro, *Zebra Stripes*, p. 150.

28 Brenda Larison et al., 'How the Zebra Got its Stripes: A Problem with Too Many Solutions', *Royal Society Open Science* (14 January 2015), http://rsos.royalsocietypublishing.org.

29 Caro, *Zebra Stripes*, p. 161.

30 Ádám Egri et al., 'Polarotactic Tabanids Find Striped Patterns with Brightness and/or Polarization Modulation Least Attractive: An Advantage of Zebra Stripes', *Journal of Experimental Biology*, 215 (2012), pp. 736–45.

31 Caro, *Zebra Stripes*, p. 175.

32 David Barnaby, *Quaggas and Other Zebras* (Plymouth, 1996), p. 83.

33 Eric Harley et al., 'The Quagga Project: Progress Over 20 Years of Selective Breeding', *African Journal of Wildlife Research*, XXXIX (2009), pp. 156–63.

34 Thomas Page and Colin Hancock, 'Zebra Cousin Went Extinct 100 Years Ago. Now, It's Back', CNN (27 July 2016), http://edition.cnn.com.

35 Ibid.

6 Z IS FOR ZEBRA

1 See www.stevensonbros.com.

2 Edward Lear produced around a dozen illustrated alphabets, many of which have been reproduced in facsimiles.

3 For the full story, see Helen M. Sidebotham, *Round London's Zoo* (London 1928), pp. 113–15.

4 Choi Du Seon, 'The Nation's Only Grévy's Zebra Dies at the Age of 31', *My Daily* (9 December 2011), www.mydaily.kr.

5 'Death of the "Bewitching Femme Fa-Mal" Grévy's Zebra', Yonhap News (7 December 2011), www.yonhapnews.co.kr.

6 Rebecca Murray, 'Interview: Hayden Panettiere Discusses "Racing Stripes"', *About Movies* (November 2005), available at www.thoughtco.com.

7 Ibid.
8 The wallpaper is still widely available, see www.scalamandre.com.
9 See Jessica Tiffin, 'Stick Becoming Crocodile: African Fairy-tale Film', in *Fairy-tale Films Beyond Disney: International Perspectives*, ed. Jack Zipes, Pauline Greenhill and Kendra Magnus-Johnston (New York, 2016), p. 231. See also C. R. King, C. R. Lugo-Lugo and M. K. Bloodsworth-Lugo, *Animating Difference: Race, Gender and Sexuality in Contemporary Films for Children* (Lanham, MD, 2010).
10 See Scott MacDonald, 'His African Journey: An Interview with Peter Kubelka', *Film Quarterly*, LVII/3 (2004), pp. 2–12. The film is widely available on the Internet.
11 For further examples, see Rachel Poliquin, *The Breathless Zoo: Taxidermy and the Cultures of Longing* (Philadelphia, PA, 2002).
12 Hirst was not the first to use actual zebras in his work. In 1973 the Italian artist Mario Merz (1925–2003) integrated a taxidermy zebra head within his sculpture *Zebra (Fibonacci)*, mixed media, 1973.
13 For further discussion, see Karen Wonders, *Habitat Dioramas: Illusions of Wilderness in Museums of Natural History* (Uppsala, 1993), pp. 170–77.
14 Websites consulted include 'Zebras R Us' www.zebrasrus.com/zebra-baby; see also 'Exotic Animals for Sales', www.exoticanimalsforsale.net/zebras-for-sale.asp; 'Lonesome Bull Ranch', www.lonesomebullranch.com/zebras-for-sale.html; www.zebrasrus.com/zebras-for-sale.html and 'Hoof Web', www.hoofweb.com/bb/sales.html.

Select Bibliography

Barnaby, David, *Quaggas and Other Zebras* (Plymouth, 1996)

Bryden, H. A., 'Zebras and their Characteristics', *The Pall Mall Magazine* (July 1896), pp. 373–84

Caro, Tim, *Zebra Stripes* (Chicago, IL, 2016)

Gall, Dolores M., '"This Most Elegant of Quadrupeds" – Illustrations of the Quagga', *Discovery* XV/2 (1980–81), pp. 44–51

Groves, C. P., and Catherine H. Bell, 'New Investigations on the Taxonomy of the Zebras Genus *Equus*, Subgenus *Hippotigris*', *Mammalian Biology*, LXIX (2004), pp. 182–96

Kingdon, Jonathan, *Mammals of Africa, Volume V* (London, 2013)

Lydekker, R., *The Horse and its Relatives* (London, 1912)

MacClintock, Dorcas, *A Natural History of Zebras* (New York, 1976)

—, 'Professor Marsh's Quagga Mare', *Discovery*, XV/2 (1980–81), pp. 34–43

Menzies, J. I., 'Man and the Zebra', *Oryx*, I/3 (Sept 1951), pp. 127–33

Ritvo, Harriet, *Noble Cows and Hybrid Zebras: Essays on Animals and History* (London, 2010)

Tegetmeier, W. B., *Horses, Asses, Zebras, Mule and Mule-breeding* (London, 1895)

Willoughby, David, *The Empire of Equus* (New York, 1974)

Associations and Websites

AFRICAN WILDLIFE FOUNDATION
www.awf.org

GREVY'S ZEBRA TRUST
www.grevyszebratrust.org

THE QUAGGA PROJECT
http://quaggaproject.org

THE INTERNATIONAL UNION FOR THE CONSERVATION OF NATURE (IUCN)
www.iucn.org

IUCN SPECIES SURVIVAL COMMISSION (SCC) EQUID SPECIALIST GROUP
www.equids.org/species.php

Acknowledgements

Zebras, with the exception of adult male Grévy's zebras, are seldom to be found alone and tend to herd together. Likewise, a book project is not a lone endeavour. The authors would like to acknowledge the kind assistance of the following institutions: the Natural History Museum in London and Tring, the Peabody Museum of Natural History, the Royal College of Surgeons, London Zoological Society Library, the Lewis Walpole Library, the Rijksmuseum and the Martin and Osa Johnson Safari Museum. Particular thanks to all the staff at the Yale Center for British Art. The following individuals kindly granted picture permissions, interviews and/or shared their expertise on the subject of zebras: Dorcas MacClintock, Tim and Rosie Holmes, Jonathan Silin, Kathi Packer, Rory Carnegie, Tim Caro, Catherine and Megan Berning, Matt Mabe, Dolly Jørgensen and Ian North. Thanks also to friends and family for all the zebra spotting, and for putting up with all the zebra talk.

Photo Acknowledgements

The author and publishers wish to express their thanks to the below sources of illustrative material and/or permission to reproduce it.

Courtesy of Ardmore Ceramics: p. 113; authors' collections: pp. 16, 50, 51, 110, 111, 116, 117, 118; permission granted by Beach House via Sub Pop records: p. 173; Bridgeman Images: pp. 48 (Pictures from History), 127 (Private Collection/© The Lucian Freud Archive), 128 (Manchester Art Gallery, UK); courtesy of the artist Rory Carnegie: p. 135; reproduced with the permission of the Colecciones Reales, Spain: p. 54; Fotolia: pp. 33 (Nico Smit), 39 (Jan Van Der Voort), 42 (Yul); courtesy of the John Paul Getty Museum: p. 59; reproduced with the kind permission of Dolly Jørgensen: p. 79; photo by Robert Giard; © Estate of Robert Giard: p. 121; reproduced with the kind permission of the Martin and Osa Johnson Safari Museum: p. 145; courtesy of the artist Matt Mabe: p. 161; courtesy of the Ugo Mochi estate: p. 130; © The Trustees of the Natural History Museum, London: pp. 95, 103, 104; courtesy of the New York Public Library: p. 61; courtesy of the artist Kathi Packer; p. 133; imocut courtesy of Samuel Shaw: pp. 24, 26, 28; courtesy of the Rijksmuseum, Amsterdam: pp. 15, 33, 34, 71, 79, 80, 81, 82, 142, 163, 181; The Royal College of Surgeons of England: pp. 96, 97; © Tate, 2008: p. 124; © Tate, 2015: p. 122; courtesy of the Victoria & Albert Museum, London: pp. 55, 119; courtesy of the Lewis Walpole Library, Yale University: pp. 63, 64; courtesy of the Yale Center for British Art, Paul Mellon Collection: pp. 68, 69, 70, 72, 76, 77, 86; courtesy of the Yale Center for British Art, Gift of Charles Ryskamp in honour of Mr and Mrs Paul Mellon: p. 6.

Index